JOHN DAVENPORT
RALLY!

Hamlyn
London·New York·Sydney·Toronto

Acknowledgements

The publishers are grateful to the following individuals and organizations for the illustrations in this book: *Autocar; Autosport;* B and B Photography; Hugh Bishop; British Leyland; Robert Clayson; Chrysler; John Davenport; DPPI; *East African Standard;* Ford; David Hodges; Lancia; Automobile Club de Monaco; Michel Morelli; *Motor;* Peugeot; Photo VB; Renault; Saab; Nigel Snowdon; Colin Taylor; Top-Foto; Peter C. Wood.

Published by the Hamlyn Publishing Group Limited
London · New York · Sydney · Toronto
Astronaut House, Feltham, Middlesex, England
Copyright © The Hamlyn Publishing Group Limited 1976

Second Impression 1977

ISBN 0 600 37570 6

Filmset in Great Britain by Siviter Smith Limited, Birmingham
Printed and bound in The Canary Islands by Litografía
A. Romero, S. A. Santa Cruz de Tenerife. Canary Islands (Spain)
D. L. TF. 677 - 1976

Contents

The Unique Sport

Competing in a rally is most exhilarating. There is all the sensation of speed that one gets while motor racing without the dangers inherent in three figure velocities. There is a feeling of adventure in that there is no constant circulation on a well-known road but rather a journey over unfamiliar terrain. There is the camaraderie of sharing the experiences with someone else in the same car, and often only overcoming problems because two heads are better than one. It does lack the wheel-to-wheel struggles of racing but this is outweighed by the broadness of its appeal and the wide range of experience that it can offer. A night on the Yorkshire Moors in a rally car can give six hours of entertainment and sufficient incidents for a couple of weeks of story telling by two people, which in this era of diminishing returns is good value indeed.

If there is one neurosis associated with rallying, it is that of feeling the 'poor man' of motor sport. The stars of motor racing find their names in the daily papers, more frequently in the social columns than in the obituary, while the aura of big money,

dangerous living and a general dolce vita hangs about them. Such fame is not the common lot of the rally driver. There are a few lauded names which are widely known outside the sport but otherwise the general public is little aware of rallying.

Consequently, there is a great temptation to talk about the sport, especially when one is closely associated with it, as if rallyists are an oppressed minority. If I were to do that it would be unfair both to the reader and to rallying—truly it is a magnificent branch of motor sport capable of standing on its own as an incomparable source of entertainment and excitement. For the competitor, a rally can be a combination of adventure and travel which makes heavy demands on his driving talents and on his ability to be competitive in a whole range of activities from bush engineering to getting the attention of waiters. The spectator is less catered for in rallying than in racing, for if he wishes to watch a rally where it is most exciting, he must perforce undertake something of a miniature rally. Nevertheless, rally spectating is on the increase and it is estimated

Preceding pages: an HRG in the 1951 Alpine Trial

Right: not the way one plans to go rallying, and sometimes spectators can be useful. Saabs are famous for regaining their feet, and Per Eklund is a modern exponent of the 'Carlsson technique'

Below: one of the most successful Porsche drivers was Vic 'the Quick' Elford, here seen with regular co-driver David Stone on the Swedish Rally of 1967. The following year he won the Monte Carlo in a similar car

that several million people watched the mid-1970s RAC Rallies of Great Britain.

When rallying first started, it was as much a spectator sport as racing, for the open road was their common area. Racing gradually acquired its permanent circuits such as Brooklands, Montlhéry and the Nürburgring and left the open road for the security of prepared tracks, though some racing in Europe still takes place on public roads especially closed for the occasion. In face of the increasing amount of road traffic, rallying became a sport of mountains like the Alps and the Dolomites. It was primarily a sport to be appreciated by the competitor, but in the post-war era this was to change as rallying in Europe became more a matter of concentrated speed tests rather than thinly disguised road races transferred to remote mountain areas. The speed test and the special stage brought back the spectator who found that he could watch derivatives of his own car performing acrobatics on rally roads.

The long-distance event did not die; it just migrated. The last of the classic road events that did not rely on special stages to give a result was the Liege-Sofia-Liege, the legendary Marathon de la Route of the Royal Motor Union of Liege in Belgium. With the perhaps unwitting aid of the Yugoslav and Bulgarian authorities, they were able to organize this event as late as 1964. It was the most highly regarded rally of its type by drivers, manufacturers and journalists, but the increase in tourist traffic rendered it unwelcome. However, in regions such as East Africa where the governments were sympathetic, the roads were nowhere near as good as in modern Europe, and local traffic still moved around on two feet, the seed of long-distance rallying took root and has flourished ever since. Indeed, the East African Safari has become a by-word

for rugged reliability in the motoring world.

Perhaps the most attractive thing about rallying is that no two events are quite the same and each event has its own unique flavour. There is, naturally, much variation in the type of road used on individual rallies and also in the terrain that they cross. Just as Corsican roads are prized as being the twistiest of the tarmac variety, so another island, Cyprus, has the highest score of sinuosity as far as dirt roads are concerned. Then there is a world of difference between a winter rally like the Finnish Marlboro Arctic which takes place north of the Arctic Circle and a rally like the Moroccan which takes competitors over the outskirts of the Sahara. There is

a constant change of scenery and, although it is sometimes remote, it is invariably spectacular. As if to match this kaleidoscope of background, the rallies do not conform to a formal pattern. A rally may be decided purely on speed tests timed to the second or, if they are long enough, as in Australia, to the minute. Or it may be that it has no speed tests at all and relies on virtually impossible average speeds set on the open road to decide the result. A rally may be gruelling for the driver who is asked to keep going for long periods without a halt for a rest, or it may be very demanding on the car by allowing no time for service and impounding the car while the driver sleeps.

The variety of events and the changing character of rallies gives plenty of freedom of expression to the participants, whether competitors, organizers or spectators. Consequently, rallying produces a regular crop of stories which are guaranteed to make even a fisherman feel that he has stumbled on a rich vein of hyperbole. The thing about rallying is that they are usually true. Spectators heave and push cars from ditches and snow banks and think it part of the fun—Hannu Mikkola once published an advertisement in a Finnish newspaper thanking the Lapps who put his car back on the road the year he won the Arctic Rally.

But no matter the variety of stories that are told about a myriad of rallies, there is a common element that makes a rally a Rally and without it the event would not be accepted as such. The Concise Oxford Dictionary gives the meaning of 'rally' as 'to reassemble and get together again' and this was certainly the way it was meant for the Monte Carlo Rally where competitors drove from different starting points to the common finishing town. However, the OED points out that the word also means 'to revive by an effort of will' and that meaning is much closer to the essence of the sport than the original derivation. Rallying essentially takes in motoring on

public roads, for longer periods than is considered conventional for normal driving. Either here or on other specially selected roads the driver and the car have to achieve certain standards of speed and durability. To help them, the car also carries a second driver, called the co-driver, whose business it is to complement the driver and make sure that the right route is followed, the right time schedule is observed and that everything possible is done to get the best from both car and driver. It is this team effort more than anything else which characterizes rallying. The crew and their car may be alone for long periods when only by virtue of their own efforts will they keep going and survive.

The challenge presented to a car and its crew may vary from a hundred miles or so of British lanes to be covered in a single night to three thousand miles of African bush roads to take up five days of hard driving. The name of the game is rallying and the basic problems are the same. The crew cannot look alongside and see how their rivals are faring and thus they must use their own judgement, aided by information gathered at rest halts and the like and backed up by their experience, to know how hard to press the car and themselves in order to gain the best result. At one and the same time they are struggling to overcome the problems of time and distance set by the organizers as well as trying not to damage their car on the terrain that must be covered. The weather too must be taken into account and sometimes that can become the most important factor of all, as on the Monte Carlo Rally of 1965 when the entire rally got caught in a blizzard. As well as all this, the rally crew must come to the finish with fewer penalties than any other crew in order to win.

It is that unique combination of problems that makes Rallying.

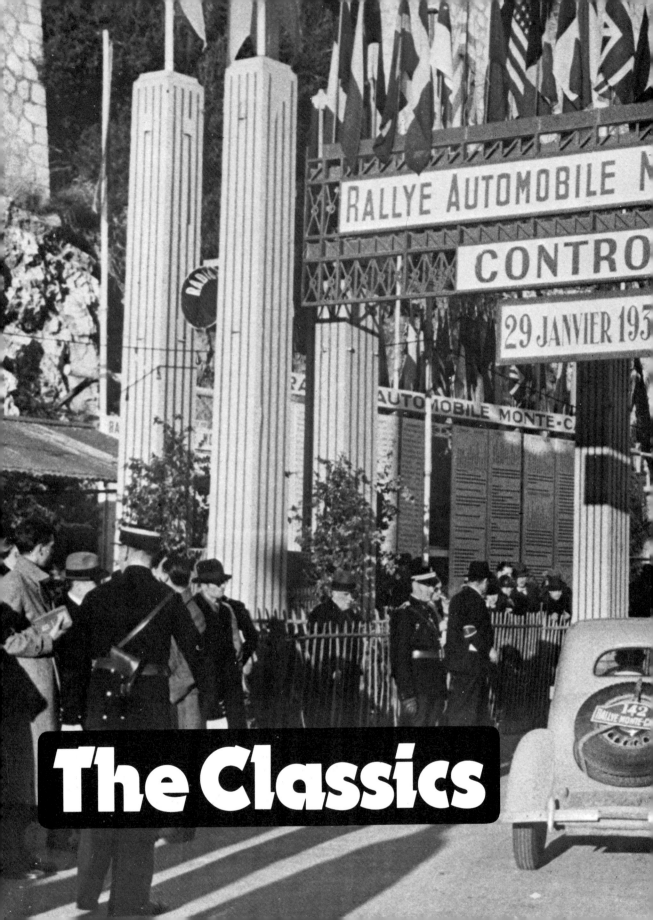

The Classics

Because of the difficulty in defining a rally, it is not easy to say which was the first such event. There is little doubt that the Monte Carlo Rally was the first motoring event to use the word 'Rally' in its title—this was due to the format of the event, then unique, in which cars started from many places and journeyed to a single destination, Monte Carlo. However, many events pre-dated this illustrious event and deserved the modern title of Rally.

The very early motor sport events were invariably called trials, largely one suspects because the organizers had no idea if any car would be able to achieve the task set. What is reckoned to be the first motor sport event was the Paris to Rouen Reliability Trial of 1894, which was followed one year later by the first proper race from Paris to Bordeaux and back. Some features of these events placed them much nearer the modern conception of rallying than racing; the cars were started at intervals, they invariably carried passengers who were not only mechanics ready to pump oil or change wheels but also assisted in finding the correct route, and the 'track' upon which the event was disputed was, naturally, the public highway. What prevents them being considered legitimate forerunners of rallying is that there was no question in these events of regulating them with time controls or of setting average speeds.

It is sad to have to recall that accidents in those early events held on the public road were quite common. More often than not, competitors suffered most in such mishaps, with dogs and chickens also rating high on the casualty list, but the seriousness of the accidents and their rate of incidence crept up as the speeds increased. Very often the technical development centred on the engines, to make cars faster, and little thought was given to such minor details as suspension and brakes.

In 1903 the Paris to Madrid race was halted before half-distance as there had been a series of incidents. As a result, racing was banned in France and although the ban was neither complete nor long-lasting, it did serve to push racing onto closed circuits. It was soon to be widely realized that on a closed circuit of roads, albeit public roads closed to other traffic for the occasion, the requirements of safety and the control of spectators could be effected far more easily than over hundreds of miles of open roads.

The appeal of the open road was not to be denied. Many racing classics continued to be run in the fashion of those pioneering events and one has only to recall the Targa Florio, the Carrera Panamericana and the Mille Miglia to realize that open-road racing did not die at once.

At the turn of the century, there were plenty of innovators around, and from those early trials another form of motor sport evolved which tested a car and its driver in ways other than sheer speed, though it must at once be confessed that no matter how many formulae were invented, in those early days it often came down to a question of time over a standing start speed test. In 1904, Germany produced the Herkomer Trophy, which was described by a contemporary source as being 'a long distance regularity contest for touring cars'. It did include speed tests but the emphasis of the competition lay in maintaining average speeds, passing through controls in the right sequence and at the correct time and in not losing the way. There are some points which a modern rallyist would recognise! The biggest problem was that in order to specify exactly those things which the competitors had to do and those that they were penalized for doing, the organizers had drawn up imposing regulations. So imposing were they that few competitors under-stood them in their entirety and were even more baffled by decisions the judges based on the regulations. Thus there was much acrimony at the finish of the rally—a situation that still occurs today when drivers and organizers place a different interpretation on the same regulation. It is only necessary to cast back as far as 1966 to find both the Monte Carlo Rally and the Acropolis Rally suffering from protests which were to delay the results for months until all the protests and appeals had been heard, or to the confused finish of the 1974 Press-on-Regardless Rally.

Perhaps because of its complicated regulations, the Herkomer Trophy did not last more than a couple of years, but the idea of such an event had been planted. The German automobile industry was very keen to have a pro-motion in which their cars could be shown at their best against competi-tion from all over Europe. In face of strong opposition from the German Parliament (in the same year measures to tax motor cars and restrict their speed had been introduced), the patron of the Imperial Automobile Club, Prince Heinrich of Prussia, brother to His Imperial Majesty Wil-helm II, was persuaded to lend his name to a competition similar to the Herkomer Trophy. It would be called the 'Prinz Heinrich Fahrt'. Frankly, he did not need much persuading to sup-port the event as he was a keen com-petition driver himself, having taken part in the 1906 Herkomer Trophy, while his eminent brother was also a motor car fanatic.

The first Prinz Heinrich Fahrt was held in 1908 and received an entry of over 140 cars, of which some 130 came to the start line. Amongst the drivers was Ettore Bugatti who had already started to build cars under his own name at Molsheim, but on this occasion was at the wheel of a Deutz. Another well known name, still cur-rent in rallying, was that of Carl Opel who did drive a car of his own manu-facture. The whole event was spread out over seven days and 1400 miles, starting in Berlin and finishing in Frankfurt-am-Main. The average speeds, set between 15 and 20mph, were determined for each car by a formula relating to the number and bore of the cylinders. The piston stroke was ignored, which led to some clever chaps building very tall engines especially for the event. There was a single-speed test on which drivers could earn bonus points by going fas-ter than their set time and a mountain test with a specified average. Four of the largest German cars crashed on this mountain test but there were plenty of more agile ones at the finish in Frankfurt; the Germans took vir-tually all the prizes, with the overall victory going to Fritz Erle in a Benz with a super-lightweight body. It is interesting to note that although there were controls to check how the com-petitors were doing, most of the penalties were noted down by an im-partial observer allotted to each car. This is unheard of today, save in economy runs, where riding observers still check that the drivers stick to the rules.

A similar event was held the next year, but German superiority was not so complete. One of the Opel brothers, Wilhelm, won outright but second was Count Kolowrat in a Laurin and Klement built in the Czechoslovak factory that was later to become Skoda. Every effort was made to ensure that in 1910 this now prestigious event would be once more a showpiece of the expanding Ger-man automobile industry. The Aus-trians, however, had other ideas. That same year they held their first Interna-tionale Alpenfahrt, which used the in-famous Katschberg Pass as its centre-piece and was to grow into one of the most famous rallies between the two World Wars. They also had the

Daimler factory where young Ferdinand Porsche was designing and building cars. With the help of one Joseph Brosch, who was later better known as Marshal Tito of Yugoslavia, he prepared three factory Daimlers for the 1910 Prinz Heinrich Fahrt. He drove one himself and won the six-day event outright, while the other two team cars were second and third. Daimler were jubilant but it was a Pyrrhic victory, for the result did little to help sales as people were a bit wary of a car which had *such* outstanding performance. Also the German press, with the backing of the parliament, weighed in with cries of 'professionalism' so that even its patron had to reluctantly withdraw his support and the event lapsed.

The Austrian Alpine, however, went from strength to strength, despite problems with organizational naivety in the early events. By the outbreak of the First World War it was an 1800 mile event based on Vienna and lasting a full week. It had 19 tests on mountain passes and penalties for servicing the cars, which were impounded every night while the drivers rested. Cars from all over Europe competed in this classic and even Rolls-Royce sent a team which, while it did not win outright, took class awards with a commendable performance.

One year after the inauguration of the Alpenfahrt, the Société des Bains de Mer at Monaco had decided that since motor cars were so popular and as their town was devoid of customers in the period from January to March, they might be able to use the former to resolve the latter. Out of this promotional idea was born the most famous rally of them all which, to give it its full title from 1911, was the 'Rallye Automobile vers Monte Carlo'. The first event, held in January 1911, was not the most rigourous of affairs as the whole idea was to get the rich motoring enthusiasts down to

Monaco where they could enjoy the sun and spend their money. Since most of the rich could afford chauffeurs the time schedules were sufficiently generous to allow halts for rest and repast while the only tests were held on the promenade of Monaco. There were 23 entries and 20 cars set out from various large towns across Europe to travel down to Monte Carlo. In Paris and Monaco, the event was followed quite avidly and there was mild rejoicing when it was revealed that a Frenchman, Henri Rougier, had won the rally at the wheel of a Turcat Méry. In the categories on which the cars were judged at the finish, he won most points in those for speed and the comfort the car offered its passengers.

From such small beginnings, great things were to come and another Monte Carlo Rally was held in 1912 but the third rally was not held until 1924. It was run in March so that it would arrive in the Principality as the Season was launched with Monte

Above: grace and space in the early days—this is Henri Rougier's Turcat-Méry in the 1911 Rallye vers Monte Carlo

Right, top: Donald Healey, one of the most famous British names in rallying, on the famous hairpins of the Col de Braus as he drove in the 1930 Monte Carlo Rally in a Triumph Super 7

Right, centre: kitchen sink era—this Sunbeam 25 equipped for the 1932 Monte has snow chains, electric screen heater and shovels

Right, lower centre: the co-driver in this 1934 photograph might have smiled at the rumpus when Munari won the Monte Carlo Rally for the third time in 1976—he is Jean Trevoux, and had just won in this Hotchkiss. He won again in 1939, 1949 and 1951

Right, lower: Berlescu demonstrates his notorious 'snow special' Ford V8

Carlo Week. Few entries were received and to all intents and purposes it was a flop. The following year it went back to January amid the snows and intemperate weather that seem to attract foolhardy sportsmen and was once again a success. Entries mounted year by year and in the 1930s it was common to find over 200 entries with at least 150 crews coming to the start. There was naturally a corresponding increase in popular interest and it was soon the best known motoring event in Europe.

As the cars and their equipment grew more and more sophisticated, it became more difficult—average speeds went up and routes to Monte Carlo were chosen more enterprisingly—but still the essence of the results was decided on tests held in or very close to Monaco. The major problem facing a competitor was first to choose a starting point which offered the best chance of an easy route and fine weather so that he could reach Monaco unpenalized, and then to do extremely well on the tests. Thus the rally could very much be a matter of luck and depend either on the choice of itinerary or a missed gearchange on the promenade. During an era when it was principally an event for rich amateurs, the analogy to a game of chance similar to those of the casino was not wholly undesirable.

The rally was won by Frenchmen, Englishmen, Belgians, Dutchmen and Rumanians, starting from points as diverse as Norway, Russia, Scotland, Greece and Rumania as well as from more conventional places like Paris. Their cars represented all the major makes of Europe and so it was not surprising that the factories themselves became interested in the publicity that could be gained from a win in the Monte Carlo. All the same, in those pre-war years there was very little evidence of outright attempts with full factory support.

There was, however, a definite trend that could be discerned in the attitude of the competitors. The rally changed very little but the drivers took it increasingly seriously. With the dropping of the Concours d'Elegance penalties, the choice of car was governed purely by lightness, performance and visibility so that the best result could be obtained on the infamous 'wiggle-woggle' test held on the Monaco promenade. The winning Ford in 1936 was hardly recognisable from the manufacturer's catalogue, so much had the body been chopped around. The drivers, Christea and Zamfirescou, had set up a replica of the test at home and practised for hours until they got it just right; their time in the test was the fastest in the rally and clinched victory for them. Professionalism was not quite on the scene but there were all the outward signs of it.

After the Second World War, the Monte Carlo Rally was revived much sooner than most events—the first event was planned in 1948 and held in the January of 1949. It featured a common route for the cars after a converging control at Paris; this proved very popular, for it stopped a lot of the muttering about different weather on different routes, and it was retained for subsequent rallies. Its formulae had become more complicated, not simpler with the passage of time. Now there was a complementary test of four laps in the mountains behind Monaco where competitors were penalized for completing the second, third and fourth laps in times which differed at all from that taken on the first lap. The equation for calculating penalties looked like something out of a book by Einstein but it appeared that this was just what the competitors enjoyed most—a challenge that was not on a par with racing round a circuit. The rally grew to the height of its popularity in the 1950s with entries regularly topping the four hundred mark. British participation was also at its zenith, spurred on by such success as Sydney Allard's magnificent win in 1952 driving a car of his own manufacture. He finished just four points ahead of a young man called Stirling Moss at the wheel of a Sunbeam Talbot.

Those were still the days of the amateur, but factory interest was increasing and with it came a great deal more interest in the rules. In 1953,

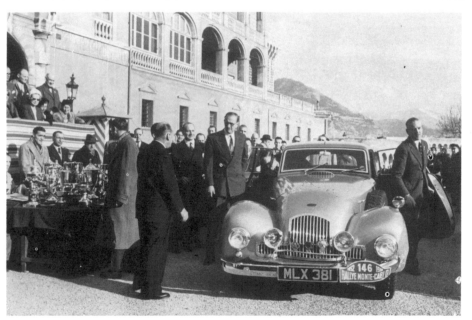

Honest mum, I built it myself. Few people could aspire to win the Monte Carlo with a car bearing their own name, but Sydney Allard did it in 1952 by just two points from a Sunbeam driver called Moss. Allard and Warburton look suitably happy at the prize giving.

French roads are always well sign-posted, and each road has its own number, so that the organizers of the Monte Carlo, for instance, only have to quote road numbers and occasional villages to define their route. This Mercedes is headed south out of Lorraine towards the Cote d'Azur in 1959

someone objected to the bodywork of certain Porsches while the following year, objections were raised to Louis Chiron's Lancia, which was claimed to have a 2-litre chassis but a $2\frac{1}{2}$-litre engine. The wrangling about his car delayed the results for no less than 10 months before it was announced that he had won; the first such victory for a Monégasque. Teams such as Rootes started to 'employ' drivers and ran a team of cars in much the same way as they would at a race meeting. Jaguar did much to help drivers like Ronnie Adams, who won the rally in one of their cars in 1956, and it was not long before other teams were formed specifically to do rallies with the Monte Carlo as the prime target. Renault and Citroen in France and Mercedes in Germany joined the fray and the development of cars and

equipment was accelerated.

One need hardly mention studded tyres as being one of the best known of these developments, but instruments for measuring distance and systems for noting down the hazards of the road in proper sequence were soon in common use, and with them the day of the amateur was over. The most powerful demonstration of this was the Monte Carlo Rally of 1960 when Mercedes went into the rally in the most excrutiating detail and their crews practised the final tests in the mountains until they were practically bend perfect, with all the average speeds noted down in terms of intermediate times. Walter Schock who headed the Mercedes 1-2-3 lost a mere 30 points in the entire rally, which was not bad when you consider that they were handed out at one per second early or late.

The rally underwent a big change in 1961 when special stages were introduced on the common run down from a converging point near Lyon to Monaco. It also produced something of a shock result as the special stage times were multiplied by a 'factor of comparison' which again looked as if it had been borrowed from one of Einstein's more obscure texts. Its implications were not immediately evident but when the results were worked out, the previously unheard-of team of Panhard Tigre PL17s filled the first three places overall. The factor of comparison lasted until 1966 but it was already clear in 1965, when Timo Makinen won in a Mini-Cooper, that a small car needed no protection from a complicated formula when the conditions were bad and the going tough. In that year, the most terrible blizzard engulfed the rally as it reached Chambéry, where the routes converged, and the special stages became a nightmare of driving in soft gluey snow with very limited visibility. Makinen emerged the victor.

That was the classic Monte Carlo Rally of the 1960s and hurried along development; today the rally is wholly decided on the scratch results of the special stages with the time controls only playing a major part in the results if the weather turns nasty or mechanical trouble intervenes. The Monte Carlo Rally has evolved to its present elevated position by virtue of the unique appeal it has offered to its competitors and the undying enthusiasm of its Monégasque organizers. It has survived two World Wars and more scandals than Madame Pompadour even dreamed about and it is still there, beloved by all who know it.

Its contemporary, the Austrian Alpenfahrt, has not been so fortunate. Between the wars, it was one of the principal events in the rally calendar and spread to cover Alpine territory in adjacent countries such as Italy, Switzerland and France. After the Second World War the idea of running a major rally through the Alps revived quickly and in 1946 a 1000 mile rally was organized by an automobile club in France and called the Rally of the Alps. The following year, Italy held a national event using the same title but in 1949 the AC de Marseille et Provence ran a full international event which took a week of motoring and covered roads in both Italy and France. One of the tests was a 113 mile run on an Italian autostrada where the police proved incapable of controlling the other traffic and many drivers were penalized because they had to lower their speed and dodge in and out between trucks. Only one car, a Citroen driven by a M.Gautruche, finished without a single penalty point and received the only Coupe des Alpes awarded.

The Coupe des Alpes as this French event was to be called, although many of its British adherents simply referred to it as the Alpine Rally, went from strength to strength. It ran into problems with the use of roads in countries like Switzerland and Germany where the authorities felt that tourism was a more important summer activity than rallying. The Swiss police used to stop competitors and talk to them for so long that they would be heavily penalized at the next control so, before long, although it remained an international event, the rally was almost entirely held in France. There were flirtations still with Italy, and an attempt to revive the Mille Miglia occurred when one stage of the Coupe des Alpes through Italy was called by that famous name; fortunately no one took it very seriously.

In its modern form, the Coupe des Alpes provided its competitors with three nights of hard motoring through the Alps of France with literally hundreds of cols and just about every backroad that the area had to offer. In order to make the event as difficult as possible, the Coupe des Alpes

The formulae used by the Monte Carlo organizers have led to some curious results, but none have been quite so surprising as in 1961, when this Panhard PL17 driven by Martin and Bateau came from nowhere to head a Panhard one-two-three. Cynical observers commented that it looked as if M. Martin was *in* a bateau . . .

organizers invented 'selectives', which were road sections of an 'especially demanding nature' where a higher average speed was set. A typical rally in the 1960s could have 50 per cent of its route classified as 'selective' with another 10 per cent given over to speed tests. A Coupe des Alpes was awarded to those competitors who had no penalty at time controls or selective controls and those who finished equal on such points were then classified according to performance on the speed tests. There was thus a world of difference between this sort of rally where the open road sections were of paramount importance, and a rally like the Monte Carlo where the focus was on special stages.

The Coupe des Alpes gained a formidable reputation among drivers and it probably shattered more reputations than it confirmed. Drivers like Jean Vinatier, Rene Trautmann, Rauno Aaltonen, Jean Rolland and Paddy Hopkirk were the intellectual kind of rallyist who could make the best of this event and pace themselves and their cars so that they would win at the finish rather than lead from the start.

The Austrian Alpenfahrt from which the Coupe des Alpes had sprung eventually reappeared on the rally scene but it achieved nothing like the success of its French offspring and it was not included in the European Championship lists until 1964. Its problems have always seemed to centre on the organization, especially for the route. Unlike most other major rallies, the route was concealed from all but the local drivers and this did nothing to encourage international participation. Paddy Hopkirk won it twice, in an Austin-Healey 3000 and then a Mini-Cooper, which did nothing to hurt its reputation, and there were signs in the 1970s that it was fast becoming ready to take its place with the best rallies of Europe until a

terrible mix-up in the 1973 event led to a storm of protests as the organizers had not accurately defined the official route; the rally suffered a crisis of organization from which at the time of writing it has not recovered.

The Coupe des Alpes is regrettably no longer with us. It too suffered a crisis of organization in 1970 and was not held that year, although a new team got the event back in 1971. The problems facing them were financial, for there was an increasing difficulty in running the traditional selectives at a time of year when tourism in the Alps was at its height; thus more use had to be made of closed roads which cost money to provide the policemen to close them. The solution was never found and this marvellous rally has disappeared from the calendar.

It joined another rallying classic, known best as The Liege but more properly as Le Marathon de la Route. Belgium may not be endowed with sufficient roads to run a major international rally but that did not stop the Royal Motor Union of Liege planning and running an event that was to prove one of the most difficult of the post-war rallies. It started back in 1931 when events were run down through Germany and Austria to the Dolomites and then across northern Italy to France and thence back to Belgium. As the event developed, it became clear that the Royal Motor Union liked rallies which were as hard on the drivers as on the car. The emphasis was on non-stop driving with extremely difficult average speeds set on all the roads. Before 1939, the pattern of the event was established with no cars finishing without penalty and several experiments from the Third Reich with drugs to keep drivers awake. It was reborn in 1951 and adopted the title of Liege-Rome-Liege which left no one in any doubt as to where it went. There was a modicum of rest for the drivers but nothing like that offered

This is what rallying in the Alps was all about. Ian Appleyard won the 1948 Alpine Trial in this SS100 Jaguar, before changing to XKs and going on to win a coveted Coupe d'Or

Two generations—a Porsche 356 and a Frazer Nash on the 1954 Alpine Trial

The only other winner of a Coupe d'Or was Stirling Moss, here on the Passo di Stelvio during the 1954 Alpine, the year he completed the hat trick. Legend has it that he finished with only two gears in the Sunbeam, which could have resulted in penalties at scrutineering and loss of the Coupe, but that some adroit work with clutch and overdrive switch during a brief road test was sufficient to convince the scrutineer . . .

27

by other classics. In 1953, Johhny Claes, who had already gained a place in the history books by being the only man ever to finish a Liege unpenalized when he won with a Jaguar XK120 in 1951, added further to the legends of the event when he drove for 52 hours non-stop after his co-driver, Jean Traesenter, fell ill. In the whole ninety hours of rallying, he had only a few hours sleep and yet his Lancia Aurelia GT was the least penalized at the finish and he won again.

The Liege organizers found that to keep its reputation they had to step up average speeds to meet the increasing capability of car and driver and this made it very unpopular in countries where roads were crowded. It last visited Rome in 1955 and subsequently went to Zagreb in Yugoslavia and finally to Sofia in Bulgaria in search of relatively deserted roads. A timing system was developed which concealed from the authorities the average speeds that were being demanded, by giving each competitor an allotted time for each section but then giving him an opening and closing time for each control as well. If one added up the allotted times, the entire rally would take one day longer than intended, so it was clear that as far as the competitor was concerned, the closing time of the control for his car was the important thing. These times were staggered for each car and the system worked very well until the penny dropped with the police.

The Liege was famous for its very straightforward attitude to rallying and this was largely due to its formidable chief, M.Garot. It was he who at the drivers' briefing one year announced that there would be secret checks to control speed and if the gentlemen would care to look at the blackboard at the rear of the room, they would find the locations of these 'secret' checks. The rally also developed the interesting system of starting cars three at a time from a control with

Hardly a car for a lady, but then Pat Moss was a very special lady, who could make a car travel faster than most drivers. She did not win the Liege-Rome-Liege in the year this photograph was taken, but finished fourth overall. It was in 1960 that, with Ann Wisdom, she took another Healey to outright victory in this gruelling event

each bunch going at three minute intervals. This added a lot of spectator attraction and was popular with the drivers of fast cars who knew that in the dust of the Dolomites, they had at least three minutes to catch up on the car in front instead of just one. The last Liege was run in 1964 when Rauno Aaltonen, once the apprentice of Eugen Bohringer, took the victory with an Austin-Healey 3000 and prevented the German ace from completing a hat-trick in the rally. The big Healey had won the Liege once before, when in 1960 Pat Moss and Anne Wisdom set the rally world on its heels by winning what was freely acknowledged to be its toughest and most arduous event.

Classic rallies are not so many these days, although it may well be argued that the RAC Rally of Great Britain which started back in 1929 as a gentleman's tour with a few driving tests thrown in and is now a full-blooded special stage event, should qualify for this adjective. The Acropolis Rally in Greece, although only born since the Second World War, should be considered in the same way, but one must look outside Europe for the one event that is undisputably a rallying classic, albeit a modern one.

The East African Safari started life as a rally to celebrate the Coronation of Queen Elizabeth II (one suspects that it was more a utilization of the holiday given for that august occasion, by rally enthusiasts who were keen to run an event anyway). The lack of tarmac roads and the unpredictable weather made a natural combination to provide the kind of adversity that is essential for a rally; the Alps have their snow and ice, the Dolomites their dust and now there was East Africa with its mud. The first Safari slithered to a halt in Tanzania and the cars did not complete the route but went straight back to the finish in Nairobi. In any other rally this would have been considered a disaster. The Safari thrived on it. As the largest sporting event in that part of the world, it received blanket coverage by press and radio and to be a 'Safari Driver' was almost as prestigious as being a Battle of Britain pilot around the bars of Nairobi, Dar es Salaam and Kampala.

Until 1957, the rally remained a parochial effort but then the organizers received an international licence and the first pilgrims started to come out from Europe, first to drive locally prepared cars and then with their own cars and teams. The Safari received more and more European entries but, try as they might, it was always a local driver there at the end with the wreath around his neck. Erik Carlsson was a legendary figure in those Safaris of the early 1960s and he led it more times in his 850cc Saab than his rivals care to recall. However, he was often to fall victim to mechanical failure or mischance, as in 1963 when he hit an aardvark when leading and damage led to his retirement. Ford were ardent supporters of the rally year after year with teams comprising both local and European drivers. They won the team prize often but not until 1964 did they win the rally outright, with a Cortina GT driven by Peter Hughes and Billy Young. They were also to have the distinction of being the first team to win the event with a European crew, but that had to wait until 1972 when Hannu Mikkola and Gunnar Palm in an Escort BDA finally achieved what so many had failed to do.

The Safari has changed little from year to year. It has always been a question of following a reasonably plain route from time control to time control with just a few passage controls to ensure that no one takes obvious short cuts. The times allowed on these road sections are generally impossible to achieve so that the essence of the rally is virtually road racing, but the length of the event, over 3000 miles in most cases, and the terrible conditions which can prevail, mean that far more is involved than going flat out, as many of the European drivers found when they first came to tackle the event. Towards the end of the 1960s, the rally organizers did try to use a higher proportion of 'main' roads but this meant putting the average speeds up, to over 90mph in places, and although the governments of East Africa are pretty helpful in suspending speed limits and the like for the duration of the rally, this was felt to be a bit much and the event has since returned to the bush tracks. An air of excitement pervades the whole event and even now, when through political causes it is run entirely within Kenya, the atmosphere is terrific. The rally traditionally takes place over the Easter weekend which allows the marshals to give their time freely and ensures that the entire nation turns out to watch the rally go by.

These are the classics of rallying. Their story is the story of the sport and wherever rallying is discussed, their names are mentioned.

The Changing Scene

A rally can be so small that it only takes a few hours in an afternoon, or so large that it will need a month from start to finish. The longest rally so far has been the 1970 World Cup Rally sponsored by the *Daily Mirror*. This covered 16000 miles in Europe, South and Central America, which represented 26 days of driving starting on April 18th and finishing on May 27th with a break in the middle while the cars were shipped over the Atlantic. As if that wasn't enough, the veteran Citroen driver, Bob Neyret, nipped over to Morocco during the rest and won the gruelling Rallye du Maroc before flying on to re-start the World Cup in Rio de Janeiro!

Events as big as the World Cup are not organized every year, as the funds needed to run them and to compete in them are not always forthcoming. Normally, international rallies are more modest and the participants are seldom required to spend more than a couple of nights at the wheel. In countries with dense traffic, there are nowadays sufficient rest halts for the driver to stay relatively fresh and alert.

No matter what the size of a rally, a competitor will recognise certain familiar things about it whatever country it is run in or whatever language the regulations are couched in. The object is to go from the start to the finish through a series of time controls at which the time of passage of the car will be recorded. In addition, probably to save the number of accurate watches he needs to provide, the organizer will run passage controls where some kind of stamp or marshal's signature will be placed on the competitor's time card to show visible proof that he has been to the control with his car. The route between the controls is usually laid down by the organizer, who can be as specific or as vague as he likes. The Austrian Alpine used to define the route by a list of place names and certain villages were designated as controls. Of course, there were problems when two adjacent villages were found to have the same name or the control marshal set up shop in the wrong village, but the organizers doubtless felt that it added a certain spice to the event.

The Coupe des Alpes organizers had a delightful way of telling competitors exactly where their controls could be found, for example 'in the village of St Pierre in front of the baker's house'. It was rough justice if St Pierre had two bakers but it was infinitely preferable to have some location within the village rather than have to hunt for it. In French rallies, defining the route is relatively simple as all the roads except the very humblest of cart tracks have numbers, thanks to the tidy mind of Napoleon. The N61 is the national road sixty-one while the D280 is the departmental road two hundred and eighty and, thanks to Monsieur Michelin, one can find all these numbers on a set of accurate road maps. Thus a list of road numbers plus a few village names will suffice to give a very accurate definition of the route, and indeed the modern Monte Carlo Rally still uses just that system in its regulations. More interesting still is the system used in Portugal where not only do the roads have numbers but, like France, they have kilometre stones and, in addition, tenth of kilometre stones which are well maintained and carry both the number of the road and the total distance from the start of the road. With these at their disposal nothing could be simpler for the organizers of the TAP Rally than to locate their controls by specifying the nearest little stone.

In Britain, where once the Romans had left we spent our time building ships rather than roads, there are no such aids to earth-bound navigation. Not only does Britain have no mileage stones but the network of lanes is not numbered and sometimes not

Preceding pages : the winning Ford Escort in the 1970 World Cup Rally

We all know that rally drivers must be gluttons for punishment, but Bob Neyret and Jacques Terramorsi seemed to take things a little too far when they used their week's 'rest' in the middle of the 1970 World Cup Rally to nip down to Morocco and win that tough desert event in this shortened prototype version of the Citreon DS21

even signposted. However, there are excellent maps provided by the Ordnance Survey and it is with these that British rallying has grown to its present elevated position. These maps are perhaps the best and most detailed in the world and points can be plotted on them with an accuracy of ten yards or so. The location of controls and thus the route of a rally can be given in the form of a string of numbers known as map references.

In countries not favoured with a Napoleonic system of road numbering nor with an army that publishes its maps, the only really reliable way to define a rally route is to supply each competitor with a series of written instructions in a 'road book'. These have to be prepared by an organizer going round the route and making notes which then become the road book. The most famous system and that which is used almost universally today is called the Tulip Road Book. The name comes from a well-known Dutch rally which used to start and finish in the flower growing area of that country. It was the first event to use a completely diagrammatic type of instruction linked to mileages. Nowadays, such road books are used in rallies all over the world as virtually no knowledge of language is needed for their comprehension.

When it comes to timing their events, organizers have even more freedom of choice. A British club rally will be timed to the minute and it is only the frequency with which controls occur, coupled with the sometimes difficult navigation, that enables

In the 1964 Coupe des Alpes, Erik Carlsson (*top*) finally got the little 850cc Saab through with no road penalties and won a Coupe, while the works Cortina GT driven by Vic Elford and David Stone (*above*) won the Touring category. All lit up and nowhere to go was the problem for the Mini-Coopers on the 1966 Monte Carlo Rally. (*Left*) Makinen's 'winning' car with its controversial spot lights. The last long distance classic in Europe was the 1964 Marathon, won by Aaltonen and Ambrose in this magnificent Austin-Healey (right)

SLAPEWATH to LOCKTON

109.12 Miles   Max. Time 3hrs. 50mins.

MAP	INTER MILES	TOTAL MILES	LOCATION		ROAD NO.	DIRECTION
			SLAPEWATH			
86	0.00	0.00	TIME CONTROL TC2		(A171)	WHITBY
	18.41	18.41			B1416	SCARBOROUGH
	0.87	19.28			B1416	SCARBOROUGH
	4.70	23.98			A171	SCARBOROUGH
93	10.05	34.03	BURNISTON		A171	SCARBOROUGH (TOWN)
	3.48	37.51				TOWN CENTRE
	0.20	37.71				TOWN CENTRE
	0.12	37.83			A64	YORK
	0.97	38.80				BRIDLINGTON
	0.13	38.98				ENTER STAGE

SPECIAL STAGE 6 - OLIVERS MOUNT

	INTER MILES	TOTAL MILES	LOCATION		ROAD NO.	DIRECTION
	5.65	44.58	COLLEGE LANE			LEAVE STAGE
	0.36	44.94				(A165)
	1.19	46.13				CAYTON

Lest they should stray. Nearly all rally organizers provide competitors with some kind of road book to help them with navigation, although the Liege was always different in that it just told you where controls were and let you get on with it as best you could. These are two modern examples from World Championship events. The Lombard RAC Rally road book (*left*) gives all the basic information needed to find the special stages, although on the extreme left is the relevant Ordnance Survey map reference—just in case . . . The Portuguese Rally book has a much more mathematical appearance. For each junction it gives the distance to the end of the section, the distance from the start of the section, the distance between junctions and the exact reading on the kilometre stone, where appropriate. And still people get lost . . .

this to give a clear result between equally matched crews. On most major events, the rally is split into 'specially timed sections' (also called speed tests or special stages). Here the timing is to the second but even then the competitor can expect to find variations. He may discover that there is a set time for a test and that if he goes quicker than that, he will be credited as having done the target time. Naturally, the rally organizer hopes that he will not go that fast, but it does happen sometimes. The more popular system with competitors is where each stage is run on scratch and each driver is credited with his elapsed time. As far as time controls are concerned, lateness is almost invariably penalized (there are excep-

CONTROLES / CONTROLS	KM		ESTRADAS / ROADS	INFORMAÇÃO / INFORMATION
	PARCIAIS / PARTIALS	TOTAIS / TOTALS		
P **3-1** 118.7km 2h22m	0,0 ... 0,2	0,0	E. Ligação	
118,5	0,2 ... 0,5	0,2	E.Ligação !!	
118,0	0,7 ... 0,8	0,7	E.Ligação / 17,2 EN 109	
117,2	1,5 ... 1,2	1,5	18,0 EN 109 / E.Ligação	
116,0	2,7 ... 0,8	2,7	E.Ligação / 1,3 EN 326	
115,2	3,5 ... 1,0	3,5	2,1 EN 326 / ESMOJÃES	
114,2	4,5 ... 3,0	4,5	3,1 EN 326	

tions even to that rule), and early arrival is sometimes subject to a penalty as well. This forces the competitor to stick pretty rigourously to the required schedule. Very often where the average speed is not demanding, competitors may arrive early and, provided that they do not enter the area of the control, they may service their cars in the time left before their due time of arrival at the control. This system does not apply to what are known as total regularity events which, for instance, constitute the majority of rallies held in North America. On these rallies, strict adherence to the set average speed is the whole raison d'être of the event. The average speed is not an exact number of miles an hour and changes quite frequently so the

Left: Ove Andersson
partnered by rallying
journalist, Gerry
Phillips, throws his
Toyota Celica GT
through Ae farm on the

1972 RAC Rally. So
well did he drive the
Toyota that he became
their development
driver and then team
manager

Above: another suc-
cessful Japanese car,
despite having a small
engine by European
standards, is the Colt
Lancer. Joginder Singh
won the 1974 and 1976
Safaris with Lancers,
and Andrew Cowan
(seen here in the car he
placed 4th in the 1975
Safari) won many
rallies in the Antipodes
with this model

co-driver becomes the most important man in the crew and sees little of the scenery as he keeps his head down, calculating furiously to make sure that the car does not arrive a second early or a second late at the secret controls that have been set up along the route.

The major British and Scandinavian rallies of today are purely special stage events where the cars and crews battle it out for seconds over special stages closed to any traffic. They then have a generous time allowance to get from the end of one stage to the start of the next. This is why many people who see a rally like the RAC Rally of Great Britain cannot understand what is competitive about it when all they see is rally cars being docilely driven along in company with ordinary traffic.

No such confusion is possible in a rally like the East African Safari. This event eschews the use of special stages and uses time controls operating to the minute coupled with high average speeds and bad roads to sort out the winner. Even the quickest crews are late and the distances between time controls are sufficiently great to ensure that there is a differential of more than a minute between the best performances. There is no pussy-footing on the Safari and to stop for whatever reason will mean time lost and a penalty. Consequently, service stops for refuelling and new tyres play as big a part in the result as they do at Indianapolis.

A similar kind of consideration applies on a rally like the Coupe des Alpes, the Monte Carlo Rally or the Greek Acropolis Rally. On these, although special stages will almost certainly decide the ultimate winner, the

Above: perhaps Hermann Melville would not have approved, for unlike Captain Ahab, Gene Henderson is a tubby cleān-shaven man. The Detroit policeman who won the 1972 Press-on-Regardless Rally in this works-prepared Jeep Wagoneer with Ken Pogue probably settled on the name Moby Dick because it was large and white

Right: rallying has a bonus for motor sport fans—it introduces them to remote and often beautiful countryside. This photograph is from the top of the Tunnel de la Clue de St Auban, popular with spectators and cameramen on the Monte Carlo Rally, as this part of the special stage always has ice on it

The first all-French
victory on the Monte
Carlo Rally for 11 years
was recorded in 1973
by this Alpine Renault
(*left*), crewed by extrovert Jean-Claude
Andruet and demure
Mlle 'Biche'. In Scan-
dinavia, this is called
yumping as they have
difficulty pronouncing
'j'. The exponent *(right)*
is Leo Kinnunen, who
finished third overall in
the 1973 1000 Lakes

road sections which link them together are quite difficult and any competitor who ignores them and spends too long on his service or has some mechanical problem can very easily find himself with a lateness penalty.

The types of rally seem infinite but for most people, their only direct contact with the sport is through the smaller events. Many top drivers and co-drivers have put themselves on the road to success while trying to find other roads on a navigational exercise run in their own backyard. It is a long way in terms of cost from a rally like that to the world-spanning marathons such as the World Cup, but one of the biggest attractions of rallying is that there are very few barriers to hold back the rallyist who aspires to the big time. Because a rally like the Monte Carlo can throw open its doors to some 300 or so entrants every year, a man who has enough money, and has finished sufficient small rallies to qualify in his own country for an international competition licence, can enter and compete against the best drivers in the world. If he has the car and the finance he can be there on the same event, on the same roads tackling the same conditions as the topliners of rallying. It is a chance that does not occur in many other sports.

In this sense, although to go rallying at all requires a certain amount of capital, the sport is a very social one. It is common to find drivers, marshals, spectators and mechanics mingling together in a way that is impossible at a race meeting. One of the reasons for the instant success of the Tour of Britain was that it brought racing drivers together in a rally atmosphere which they found most congenial! The same thing applies to people of different nations who seem to get on much better together when brought into that situation by a rally. The many events held behind the so-called Iron Curtain in

the 1960s were extremely popular with West European crews and did much to de-fuse the cold war by showing that motorists could circulate as freely in those countries as in their own. Perhaps the best example of this kind was the relationship, albeit temporary, established between India and Pakistan in order to run the 1968 London to Sydney Marathon through their common border. This had been closed for years to all but certain international traffic and when the rally cars went through, the border officials met and talked for the first time since the conflict had begun. The 1970 World Cup achieved similar miracles of detente in that the governments of two warring nations in Central America were persuaded to move the battle front, complete with real artillery and bullets, to give a clear passage for the rally cars.

However, the very fact that the majority of rally routes use public roads means that on occasion there must be some conflict of usage between the rallyman and Mr Everyman. The small rallies in Britain, for example, cannot avoid other traffic completely, nor can they totally avoid passing houses where people are try-

Above: wide track and low stance made the Fiat 124 Abarth Spyder a force to be reckoned with on rallies where drivers can practice on stages, but the car proved less suitable for rallies like the Lombard RAC Rally. Even Rauno Aaltonen, the original 'Flying Finn' was hard pushed to keep this car in the top ten of the RAC Rally

Right, above: in contrast to the Fiat Abarth, the Saab 96 is much higher and has a narrower track. Despite this—or perhaps because of it—Stig Blomqvist and the Saab are matchless performers in Scandinavian rallies, and consistently high on the scoreboard in Britain, as on this 1972 RAC Rally where the combination finished second overall

Right: sports cars are out of fashion in Europe—at least for rallying—but are popular elsewhere, for their good performance available at low cost. This MGB is competing in the Heatway Rally in New Zealand

Following pages: the Portugese Rally was sponsored by the TAP airline for many years, but drivers found ways of flying that did not involve buying an airline ticket. This local Opel Ascona was one of several sponsored by the Lisbon General Motors agent, but when he found that GM did not officially approve of competition motoring he gave up motor sport

France, public roads can by law be closed for speed tests, but this is not always popular. The Criterium des Cevennes passes through a part of France where the agrarian economy is fairly depressed and once the rally was welcomed by walls daubed with slogans 'give us work, not rallies', while during the event broken glass and nails were strewn in the roads.

The big internationals normally generate so much interest through publicity on television, radio and in the press that objections are often forgotten. With an event like the Monte Carlo, it is a cachet for towns or villages to have it pass through and it is not unheard of for mayors to lobby the Automobile Club of Monaco to get the route altered in their favour. The publicity attached to a major rally has also been important to the national tourist organizations of countries like Spain, Morocco, Portugal and Greece, which have been quick to see that a rally will not only bring trade to hotels and garages in the off-season but will also promote the attractions of their country back in the home of the competitors.

Running a major rally today can involve the organizer in far more than choosing a route, drawing up the regulations and getting the marshals in the correct places at the right times. He will probably have to deal with a major sponsor for his finance and then arrange for some of this to be piped off to ensure the presence at his rally of foreign competitors from a selection of countries, plus an attendant bevy of journalists to make sure that their doings do not go unreported in their local press and on television. The whole thing owes much to Barnum and Bailey, but the ballyhoo is very necessary.

Rallying has come a long way since the early events when amateur engineers and drivers pitted their skills against what often seemed like insurmountable tasks.

ing to sleep. The lengths to which British organizers go to avoid problems is amazing; they will often visit every dwelling adjacent to the route of their event and move the route away from anyone who objects. It is clear that only a certain amount of this kind of usage can be allowed and it is now carefully regulated by the law of the land.

This example can be extended to cover almost any country and, as a general principle, the amount of work necessary to prepare for the coming of a rally goes up in proportion to the density of the population of the area through which it is to run. In

The Rules of the Game

The early rallies were normally models of simplicity. In the Alpenfahrt, the challenge was basically one of surmounting various mountain passes up which the car was not really designed to travel. Those who consistently reached the top and were able to drive down the other side had done more than any man could expect and were suitably rewarded. Until quite recently, Alpenfahrt gold and silver medals were awarded to drivers who got round without more than a certain penalty. The same sort of thing motivated the organizers of the Coupe des Alpes who used to award cups, the Coupes of the title, for unpenalized performances on the road sections of their event. Very few of these coveted awards were made each year, yet there were some exalted drivers who won a gold Coupe for three such runs in successive years, or a silver Coupe for three in any number of years. Stirling Moss was the recipient of a gold Coupe for his drives in Sunbeam Talbots while Ian Appleyard was the only other man to win one driving another British car, Jaguar. Paddy Hopkirk finally won a silver Coupe when he won the rally in 1967 with a Mini-Cooper while the French driver René Trautmann won so many individual Coupes at various times that he has two silver ones.

To drive and stay in time at the controls was the basic business of the rally driver, but soon major events played around with formulae to try for 'equality' by levelling out such diverse things as cylinder capacity of engines, the number of cylinders, the all-up weight of the car, and even the number of passengers. There was hardly a rally run before the Second World War that did not have some formula bristling with square root signs and strange symbols that attempted to allow cars to compete on equal terms. What brought most of these efforts to a bad end was the fact that such formulae could be examined by the competitors before the rally and, if they were clever enough, they could take advantage of them by preparing a car which best suited the imposed handicap.

The Monte Carlo Rally experimented a great deal with these artificial equalizers. In 1966, the AC de Monaco put such a big handicap on sports cars and tuned saloon cars that it was clear well before the event took place that it would be won by a standard touring car as defined in the international regulations, Appendix J, Group 1. Problems came thick and fast upon the well-intentioned organizers for the international rules were late being published and could only be found, in French, among the regulations for the Le Mans race. Just what they were doing there, no one quite knew, but their discovery raised as many questions of interpretation as it solved. The major British factories got together and sent representatives to Paris where they put their points to the law-makers themselves and came away apparently satisfied that they knew what they were doing. As could have been foreseen, the entries for the rally comprised mainly Group 1 cars, although naturally factories like Porsche which did not make that kind of car had to be content with entering in the higher groups. The final result was that the BMC Minis finished in the first three places, Roger Clark was fourth in a Group 1 Lotus Cortina and Rosemary Smith won the Ladies Prize with a Group 1 Hillman Imp.

The Monte Carlo organizers thought that they smelt a rat; how could these standard British cars be so quick? Citroen and Lancia also had their doubts and the result was that the scrutineers decided to strip down these cars and find out if they complied with their forms of recognition, the car's 'international passport'. They could not find any dimension or measurement that was not in accordance with those on the form, allowing

of course for manufacturing tolerances. Having gone so far, it was difficult to admit that they could find nothing, so they fell back on something that they had discovered earlier, which was the use of the fog lights on the British cars as a dipped beam for the headlights which were only fitted with a single filament halogen bulb. The five cars were excluded from the rally and Pauli Toivonen of Finland was declared the winner in a Citroen. The British press was full of the scandal and published pictures of Citroen mechanics changing headlamps before their car's arrival in Monaco with captions alleging that the French cars had used the same illegal system. The British teams protested and the appeals went to Paris where they were turned down by the same august body that had ratified

Mais monsieur, your filaments are single where they should be double. The Monte Carlo scrutineers were sure that there was some foul play with the winning Mini-Cooper S in 1966, but despite stripping the cars to the last nut and bolt they had to fall back on the lighting system to find a reason for disqualification

the use of the lamps in the first place, in French of course.

Needless to say, this formula favouring Group 1 cars was not retained and there was such a hubbub that formulae have never again played a part in determining the Monte Carlo results. An equally bold experiment in 1967 limited the number of tyres that each car could use during the rally. This was an excellent idea which worked reasonably well in practice even if it did take up quite a lot of time and manpower. Each car was restricted to eight tyres for each of the two mountain sections which rather took away the advantage of powerful cars (previously these would have taken new tyres for each test). There was no handicap between the classes and all the tests were run on scratch. All the sixteen tyres were branded with a special mark and the competition number of the car and on each lap it had to carry its eight tyres at all times, so there was also a bit of a weight handicap. Marshals checked that the tyres were correct before each test. Surprisingly, for such a complicated idea, it worked out well and gave one of the closest results for years in which Rauno Aaltonen's Mini-Cooper beat Ove Andersson's Lancia Fulvia by just eleven seconds, with Vic Elford's Porsche in a very close third place. There were evident drawbacks, such as when Simo Lampinen punctured one of his precious tyres going up Mont Ventoux and drove on the puncture until the tyre parted from the rim and went over the edge. He had a lot of explaining to do to convince suspicious marshals that this was truly what had happened to the missing tyre and only the worn out rim eventually convinced them. The complications of this system caused it to be dropped, and since then the Monte Carlo Rally organizers have not tried any more controversial experiments, although they did insist in the 1976 event that each car should use the same type of tyre throughout, with no limitation on studs.

Modern rallies depend on speed tests or special stages to decide the results, although lateness at time controls and other infringements of the rules can affect the classification as well. This is largely because it is more convenient to concentrate the really fast work of the event on a limited number of roads which are closed to other traffic. Here, if there is no formula to worry about, the competitor goes as quickly as he can against the clock. Because of this emphasis on speed, most serious competitors take a leaf out of the Mercedes book of 1960 and make a reconnaisance of the roads which will comprise tests or stages. This is only possible on those rallies where full details of the routes are published beforehand and which use roads with public access for the tests. The Tulip Rally organizers used to try to keep the location of speed tests secret by only giving out the detailed route just before the rally started. Most of the tests were in France and Belgium and the local police had to know which roads were to be closed and thus the information did not stay secret for very long. A similar situation used to pertain in the Swedish Rally in the 1960s. The Swedish police are a pretty incorruptible lot but they used to get phone calls from firms asking if it was permitted to take a particularly large lorry along such-and-such a road on the date of the rally and if the police refused permission, then the cat was out of the bag.

Before leaving the subject of formulae and the Tulip Rally, it is worth recalling the system used to determine the winner of this very pleasant Dutch event. In the 1960s, it was decided on class improvement which was calculated by how much the winner of a particular engine capacity class was ahead of the second in that class; the class winner with the biggest percentage improvement won the rally outright. It so happened in 1961 that Triumph had a team of Herald coupes in the Tulip and, as the rally neared its conclusion, they calculated that by withdrawing all but their class winning car, then that car would win easily by virtue of having the biggest percentage over the second car in its class. Thus Tiny Lewis became a by-stander and Geoff Mabbs went on to win the rally for Triumph. After that caustic experience, the Tulip system was changed, to compare each class winner with the class winner on each side, but this too had its ups and downs. Rosemary Smith drove well in the 1965 rally but she was probably surprised to win outright, the result of her Hillman Imp having to be compared with the largest of the saloon classes, which in that year had no really competitive cars.

Every rally has its road sections which start and finish with time controls and, on most European events, such sections are reasonably easy to drive in time. The weather can play its part but normally the sections which link the speed tests and special stages are possible to drive without lateness penalty. This was not always so and on rallies in countries like Poland, Czechoslovakia, Rumania and Hungary, it was possible to find quite long road sections in the night which required the sort of driving normally restricted to special stages. These rallies very often used to allot different driving times for the various classes so that small engined cars had longer to reach the time controls than the bigger ones. In part, this explains how the Polish driver Sobieslaw Zasada was able to gain such amazing results on these rallies with his 650cc Steyr Puch. He won the Polish Rally outright in 1964, beating Erik Carlsson's all-conquering Saab as the class up to 700cc had longer to complete the road sections than the one from 701cc to 850cc in which the Saab competed. Zasada proved conclusively that a good little 'un is hard to beat and his very reliable Puch went on to finish so consistently in its class and in the general classification of the championship rallies that he won the title of European Rally Champion in Group 2 in 1966.

This business of having different standards for various cars was relatively easy for the regular competitor to understand, but the general public found things confusing and since something which is confusing is very little value from the point of view of publicity, a lot of pressure was brought upon rally organizers from within the sport to run things in a more straightforward manner. The general trend of rallying during the last decade has been towards simplification, especially in the critical matter of deciding who has won the rally. Thus most rallies run now on a scratch basis with no handicap between cars of different types and sizes. While it would be palpably unfair to run such a rally if it comprised merely a series of tarmac hill-climbs, it was soon apparent that, on the back roads so beloved of rallies, small cars could hold their own with the bigger ones. No better demonstration of this was needed than Erik Carlsson's three consecutive victories on the RAC Rally from 1960 to 1962 when no kind of handicap or formula was applied to the stage times.

Timing and navigation fall into the domain of the co-driver in a rally car and can play as big, or as small, a part in what goes on in the rally as the organizer decides. There are events run in Scandinavia which go under the general term of 'orienteering' in which the route follows roads of all descriptions including some which are no more than footpaths through the forest. In these events, navigational accuracy is essential to finding the well-concealed controls and thought must be given to accurate timing while at the same time guiding the driver and car through a network of tracks.

A similar but more lighthearted event run in England is the Hants and Berks Night Experts Trial on which timing is relatively unimportant but navigational accuracy and a sense of fun are essential. Here the main controls and marshals are pretty simple to find but each has a subsidary marshal who is well hidden. His location is concealed in a rhyming clue of the type used in treasure hunts and there are several decoy marshals at each place set up to lure the inaccurate off course. A time limit is set to find the genuine marshal, who has on one occasion been in a boat moored in the middle of a canal tunnel, while on another the marshal was upstairs at a party in flagrante delicto with a charming partner. In the first case, a rubber dinghy was available to reach the marshal, while in the second and more interesting case, most rallyists challenged the man only to be rejected and retire in embarrassment not realising that the young lady was the person they sought.

The run-of-the-mill club rally in Britain requires more driving skill than an event which gets its result principally by navigational and other tricks, but there is still a high emphasis on the skills of the co-driver. He will have to deal with a route plotted on an Ordnance Survey map and no matter how much the car is getting thrown around, it is his duty to 'read' the route out to the driver. It is not surprising that novices often suffer from car sickness! In this way, the co-driver can contribute a great deal to the success of the partnership and can help the driver to go faster than he would without such information, or, if not faster, then certainly a little safer. There are many ways in which the details of the route can be given out to the co-driver. He can get the whole thing an hour or so before the start of the rally, in which case he has time to reflect a little on the shortest way between controls. The route information can, on the other hand, be thrust in through the window on the start line. This exciting procedure is nicknamed 'plot and bash' and it is sometimes made even worse by only giving the location of one control when the car arrives at the previous one—this keeps both crew members on their toes all the time. By far the easiest way of giving out the route is to use map references for the controls, but if an organizer wants to put the onus even more upon the labours of the co-driver, he can dress them up in more complicated forms. Perhaps the best known of these is the straight-line diagram which looks like a discarded fish skeleton and must be read in conjunction with the map.

Of course, events of this type call for maximum improvisation on the part of the crew as just about everything from the route to the timing of the rally comes at them unexpectedly. In contrast, a special stage event held on roads when practice is not permitted puts the element of improvisation almost wholly with the driver. It is his skill that leads to success or failure; the co-driver concerns himself purely with seeing that the correct route is followed, that the marshals give the correct time and that the car receives proper service and does not lack petrol. He only comes into his own during a stage if there is an incident and someone has to get out and push.

Competitors in rallies using public roads for their stages must be expected to have prior knowledge of these stages. Those who have the time and money go out and drive over the roads themselves, while others use notes made by the more fortunate ones. In these events, the co-driver assumes a greater importance once again as he has to take in charge the matter of assessing the severity of the route and making detailed navigation notes. In addition, he will have to copy down in the form of pace notes the bend-by-bend description of the special stages given to him by the driver. During the rally, he will have to co-ordinate all this paperwork and read it back to the driver. Improvisation is never completely eliminated by such preparation and it would be wrong to think that the driver just sits there and drives according to what the co-driver is telling him. The pace notes are just an impression of the road and are extremely subjective, to say the least. The grading of bends can often be in error and though there is nothing to worry about if they have been graded too slow, the driver may have to call on all his resources to deal with those that have been graded too fast.

A rally organizer has such liberty in organizing the trivial matters of his event that a crew has to be very careful when doing an event for the first time that they understand how everything functions. On Italian rallies, the cars were timed when they crossed a line in the road opposite the marshal. To be sure that there was no error in the marshal's clock, the co-driver usually walked—or ran—to the control table while the car remained well outside the control zone. This was a good system as it meant that if a car was running late, it could just be driven straight to the control and have the time recorded immediately. There are problems associated with it and most rallies prefer the present system adopted by the World Championship events where a car may go into a control a little early and the time of passage is only recorded at the instant when the co-driver hands over the time card.

The Poles had a timing system similar to the Italians and they tried to be extra-helpful to the competitors by having a set of numbered cards hung at each time control which the

marshal was supposed to turn over every minute so that the time shown on the cards corresponded to that on his clock. These cards were visible from well over a hundred yards away and when they were accurate, the idea worked well. However, the marshals were often distracted by having to check a car in and then forgot to turn over the next minute and so turned over two at once, which was very disconcerting for the crew waiting patiently for the missing minute. There was another problem with this business of timing the car when it came into a control zone, for rallies like the old Acropolis used to have a distance of two hundred yards between the control table and the end of the waiting zone. If a co-driver was to run up and check every clock with over sixty time controls, he would cover more than seven miles. In addition, the controls were so cunningly sited that it was impossible to see the control table from the waiting car so the co-driver had to run back to signal for the driver to advance. One ingenious Frenchman solved this problem of the extra seven miles by purchasing a whistle and summoning the driver as if he were a sheep dog.

The efforts of the governing body of motor sport, the Commission Sportive Internationale, to try and standardize procedures on major rallies have met with quite a lot of success. Already there is an agreed standard for control signs which has been adopted worldwide while the basic penalties for loss of time are the same in all World Championship rallies. The main problem is that no two rallies are ever quite the same and different problems have to be solved. One thing that the CSI do insist upon is that all pertinent rules should appear in the regulations for each rally to minimise the need for cross-reference to other national regulations. Also any instruction given to rally crews should be in writing and in at least two lan-

The rules of a rally normally control only what may be done to prepare the basic car, so depending on the importance of the event and entrant's budget, unlimited service facilities can be put out on the route. At this Datsun service point at St Sauveur sur Tinée during the 1972 Monte Carlo Rally, the mechanics have roped off an area to ease their work on the 240Z of Aaltonen and Todt

guages, one of which should be the official language for the event. The lack of this can be critical. For example, in the 1964 Liege-Sofia-Liege crews were handed a piece of paper when they arrived at a control on the Adriatic coast of Yugoslavia towards the end of the first night of hard rallying. Previously, the next section had been a relatively easy one up to Zagreb and already the co-drivers were taking over from the tired drivers.

Most of them realized at once that the paper was detailing a diversion and thought that there would be an extension of time for the longer route. That was not the way of the Liege. The truth dawned on Tony Ambrose when the works Healey he was driving was passed by the Citroen team going hell for leather towards Zagreb, so he swapped seats with Rauno Aaltonen and the race was on. Their car was the least penalized in Zagreb,

equal on points with Bohringer's Mercedes, and they went on to win the event—but it was a close call.

There is a great deal of modern equipment at the disposal of rally organizers today. Many use computers to keep track of the results and make sure that both the competitors and press know exactly what the situation is as the event progresses. There is no rally which as yet has its clocks feeding straight into a computer bank, but the nearest thing to it was achieved on the Austrian Alpine where the army helped out the organizers by stationing one of their radio-telex vans at the end of each

special stage. Thus when the competitor stopped to have his finish time recorded, the army immediately tapped out both that and his start time and within seconds they had appeared on the telex machine back in Rally HQ outside Vienna. It is regrettable to have to record that not all rallies are run that efficiently and the weak link is, more often than not, the human being who reads the watch. By far the most common error in timing rally stages to the second occurs where the competitor arrives at the finish towards the end of a minute. The marshal operates the stopping mechanism for the second

One of the last examples of a car winning a major rally on handicap came in the 1966 Polish Rally, when the 970cc Cooper S of Tony Fall and Atis Krauklis defeated the 1275cc Cooper S of Timo Makinen and Paul Easter. Here the mighty midget checks in at a control

A bird in the hand may be worth two in the bush, but how about three in a Maxi? Ginette Derolland runs to check in at a control in South America during the 1970 World Cup, while Rosemary Smith and Alice Watson remain in the car, with which they won the Coupe des Dames

sweep-hand and confidently reads off the seconds before looking to see what minute should be recorded. By the time he looks at the minute hand, which never stops moving, it has passed into the next minute and so that is the one that he records. Only the rawest novice should be caught out by this, but many times co-drivers who should know considerably better have fallen for it and only notice after they have left the control. The way to get such a thing changed is to descend at once and point out the mistake *before* the clock has ticked round to the time which has been recorded on the time card. The CSI is very keen to have all rallies timed by printing clocks but in the past these have proved fragile while the new solid-state ones are prohibitively expensive to hire and insure. Eventually some economic solution will be forthcoming and when it does, perhaps we can have the whole thing tied into a computer to eliminate human error, but a lot of interest and drama will go at the same time.

Drivers

There is no standard mould from which rally drivers are produced. When a journalist is trying to summon up a suitable adjective to describe someone who has just won a major rally, the one he chooses will probably owe more to the event than to the driver. Thus anyone who has won Finland's 1000 Lakes Rally, the annual rallying Grand Prix, must be 'electrifyingly' fast and yet Hannu Mikkola who has won it five times has also proved capable of winning long distance events such as the Safari and the World Cup from London to Mexico. By contrast, Eugen Bohringer was dubbed 'tenacious and enduring' when he won the Liege-Sofia-Liege twice for Mercedes, but he had also won the Acropolis Rally which was decided principally on special stages, while the same year he also came second on the Monte Carlo which is a test of speed if nothing else!

Thus it would be fair to say that, while specialists do exist in rallying, the top drivers are generally all-rounders who can do as well on an event like the Safari as on a Monte Carlo. Evidence, if any was needed, is provided by the institution of the seeding system of the CSI which grades rally drivers and gives the accomplished ones the right to start first in all FIA recognised rallies all over the world.

A man who has done much to lift the image of the rally driver into the focus of the public eye is Erik Carlsson. For over a decade, the big Swede in his small 850cc red Saab caught the imagination of the general public, first in his home country, then throughout Europe and finally worldwide. He is retired now from active participation in rallying and divides his time between travelling round the world acting as a public relations man for Saab and being with his family. Since he married Pat Moss in 1964, they have become the first family of rally-

ing and their daughter Susie is going to find it hard to find interests in other sports when she grows up.

Carlsson was born in Trollhättan, the Swedish town where the Saab aeroplane factory was to start producing cars after the Second World War. Initially, the young Carlsson's interests lay with motor bikes and he was later to attribute much of his excellent car control on loose surfaces to his early experiences with the bikes which often brought him into intimate contact with the road. To be successful in competition on a motor bike, one must be instantly aware of any change in surface or condition or one may find a closer inspection taking place. Carlsson left the army in 1949 and almost at once became interested in cars. He competed in a few rallies, which were all the rage in Sweden at that time, but it was not until 1953 when his employer persuaded him to act as his co-driver that the bug bit really hard. He saw that he could drive at least as quickly as his boss and purchased a Saab 92 with which to prove this theory.

He had some modest successes and very soon one thing led to another. Carlsson built up connections with the Saab factory and, as his success grew, he was offered special parts to be tried out as development for competition purposes. From this, it was but a short step to employment by the firm as a test driver and he formally joined Saab in 1957. Part of the job was to drive a works prepared Saab in rallies and he threw himself into both parts of the job with great enthusiasm. So great was his verve that he soon earned the nickname of 'Erik på taket' which means 'Erik on the roof', but his rallies did not always finish up like that and soon his ability to drive in such a 'crazy' fashion without having an accident established him as the best driver in Sweden. His first event outside Scandinavia was the Tulip Rally of

Preceding pages: Erik Carlsson arriving at the Mikese control in the 1966 Safari

Right, top: the Turini in daylight? And so few spectators? It is difficult to reconcile this 1964 shot of Erik Carlsson and Gunnar Palm heading for third place at Monte Carlo with the furious activity up on that famous hill in these more rally-conscious times

Right, lower: the rallying Carlssons. One might be forgiven for thinking that Pat and Erik were built for comfort rather than speed behind the wheel, but these two were dominant in rallying for half a decade

1957 and his first big international win was the 1000 Lakes Rally of the same year. At home in Sweden he was five times national ice racing champion for ice racing is to the Swedes what rallycross and autocross have become in Britain—proving and testing grounds for rally drivers and rally cars.

Carlsson won the German Rally of 1959 and the RAC Rally of Great Britain in 1960 and these important successes served to thrust the small red Saab and its large benevolent driver into the sporting press of Europe; within twelve months, everyone had heard of Carlsson and his Saab. He was to complete a hat-trick of wins on the RAC Rally, which helped to establish the Saab as one of the most popular imported cars in Britain, but perhaps even more significant for Saab sales was his record on the Monte Carlo Rally.

In 1961 he drove an estate car on the Monte Carlo as that was the only production Saab at that time to possess a four-speed gearbox. It also gave him a good Factor of Comparison from the formula in use at that time but it was not as good as that for the little French Panhards, but for which Carlsson would have won the rally outright (he was fourth but at least Saab had learnt how to go about winning). Next year, there was no mistake and he swept home to a great victory, defeating the Mercedes works driver, Eugen Bohringer, and the ebullient Paddy Hopkirk in a factory entered Sunbeam Rapier. Bohringer and Carlsson fought all year for the coveted title of European Rally Champion, which the German finally took at the end of the season by just two points. Carlsson was to repeat his win on the Monte in 1963.

Throughout the 1960s, Erik Carlsson was the best known and most successful of rally drivers. He often set himself personal targets which he sometimes failed to achieve, but in the attempt to realise them, his performance was never less than great. He wanted very much to win the East African Safari on which he finished sixth at his first attempt in 1962. That time the Saab was running at the end of the rally with no rear springs and, indeed, his Safaris always seemed to have some sort of mechanical drama associated with them. He came second in 1964 after rolling the Saab out of thick mud when it was bogged down and he and Gunnar Palm even went so far as to demonstrate the technique to sceptics during the rally ball.

Perhaps more than anything else, Carlsson wanted to win the Liege-Sofia-Liege, the old Marathon de la Route. It was a rally on which he excelled, revelling in the long distances, high speeds and the necessity for the driver to be at a peak of fitness. He came close to realising his wish but every time he found a larger and more powerful car getting home in front of him. In 1963, the order was Mercedes followed closely by Saab with Carlsson matching his 850cc saloon against the 2·3-litre sports car of Bohringer. That same year, Rauno Aaltonen was leading in an Austin-Healey until he crashed in a horrifying accident high in the Italian Dolomites but no pressure exerted by Carlsson could get the Mercedes driver to commit a similar error. The following year, Carlsson had an improved Saab and tried even harder; this time he finished ahead of Bohringer, who had won the two previous events but Aaltonen too was back with a better Austin-Healey and he went through to win outright. As this was to be the last proper Marathon de la Route held on open roads, Carlsson's ambition was thwarted for ever.

To win a Coupe des Alpes on the French Alpine Rally was a prime ambition of all rally drivers, and to win one for an unpenalized run with an 850cc car was practically impossible—but no one had told Carlsson.

He tried many times but most of the time luck was against him. In his first attempt, the car seized its engine on the way from parc fermé to the start and then in 1963, despite the most careful preparation, he missed a turning on a back road behind Grenoble and was late at a time control. A man of less determination might well have given up but the next year he returned with the familiar red car and won his Coupe, finishing second overall in the Touring Car category to do so.

Today, works Saabs have forsaken the traditional red and appear in rich yellow or lime green. They are powered by four-stroke engines emanating from another manufacturer and are still remarkably successful as the rally results of drivers like Stig Blomqvist, Per Eklund and Simo Lampinen testify. However, the corporate image of Big Erik and his Little Saab can only be recalled in conjunction with a red car emitting unfashionable clouds of smoke and making the distinctive two-stroke clatter. Indeed, the evocative nickname given these cars by their drivers of 'jungle drum with oil heating' summed them up quite well. They are missed from the current rally scene.

Arch-rival of Carlsson and equally much a gentleman was Eugen Bohringer, of whom we have already said much. A bigger contrast in styles could probably not be found—the Swede was tall and burly, the German was short and stocky and since he drove a Mercedes, which is a big car, the only parts of him that showed were the top of his head and his hands on the wheel. When he was driving the 300SEL on rallies in 1964, some people swore that he viewed the road ahead through the spokes of the steering wheel and not over it. Whatever the details of his technique for driving large cars with such a small frame, Bohringer was a very accomplished rally driver with his heart and his foot in the right place.

The most amazing thing about him was that he did not start rally driving until he was past thirty-five years of age. Born in 1923, he spent many years after the Second World War in Siberia as a guest of the Russians and it was not until some ten years after the war that he returned to his home town of Stuttgart. Once he was settled down, his attentions turned to hill climbing and racing cars. He started out with a Porsche and did well enough for the factory to give him some advice. However, it was to be the other motor manufacturer of his home town that was to introduce him to rallying for when he won races at the Solitude Ring, it occured to Mercedes that he might be just the man to drive their car in the forthcoming Lyons-Charbonnieres Rally, which started at Solitude and had a race on the circuit as its centre-piece.

His first year with them was in 1960 when his team mate Walter Schock became European Rally Champion after winning the Monte Carlo Rally. Bohringer was second overall on that event, which was not too bad for a first timer, and to rub it in he went on to win a Coupe in the French Alpine Rally. He did not do many rallies that year but in 1961 with Schock retiring from active participation, it was the gentle, balding thirty-eight year old who was groomed for the champion's rostrum. The best laid plans of mice and men...may well go astray and they did for Mercedes in 1961 for the title went to another German driver, Hans Walter who drove for Porsche. Bohringer pressed him hard and won the Polish Rally, was second on the German Rally and finished fourth overall on both the Acropolis and Tulip rallies. In winning the Polish event, Bohringer admitted that he knew little enough about loose surface driving and took along Rauno Aaltonen as co-driver, who drove the loose stages and showed him how it was done

Finnish style. In gratitude, Mercedes lent young Aaltonen a car for the 1000 Lakes Rally which he won for them but when the pair teamed up again for the RAC Rally, Bohringer left the road and the canny Mr Walter took the title.

If 1961 had been a disappointment in some ways, the next year was to be one of those seasons that other drivers just dream about. Bohringer, in his third season of rallying, was second overall on the Monte Carlo and won the Polish, the Acropolis and the Liege-Sofia-Liege outright. He nearly won the German Rally as well but Pat Moss defeated him with the relatively new Morris Mini-Cooper after Mercedes had miscalculated how fast Bohringer had to drive to get the best out of his handicap. To ruin the thing completely, it rained on the last test and thus the time which he should have recorded in order to win was just impossible. Still, by the end of the year these results had confirmed him as the new European Rally Champion. He still came to try his luck on the RAC Rally and get more experience at driving on unseen roads. He took with him Brian Culcheth, now a works driver in his own right, but repeated his effort of the previous year by leaving the road and felling a tree with the Mercedes.

The following year, Mercedes did very little competition but they did send Bohringer out with one of their new 230SL sports cars, in which he won the Liege-Sofia-Liege in fine style. He failed to win his hat-trick when he finished third with a similar car in 1964 behind Aaltonen and Carlsson but two wins and third place are a pretty impressive record. The factory entered him on several rallies with the big 300SE saloon, and he won the Acropolis Rally with such a car in 1963, but they were less successful when they made an attempt on the East African Safari in 1965. Bohringer was one of three works

drivers on that event and before the start, the local drivers were tremendously impressed with the standard of preparation and the speed of the cars. However, victory in the Safari belongs to the team with experience and Mercedes lost Bohringer when he got the big car stuck in mud.

By now, the 'newcomer' was thinking of retiring. Mercedes had stopped virtually all their competition activities, although they still retained Bohringer's services. For this reason, he was never able to accept Stuart Turner's offer of a works Austin-Healey, but Mercedes did relent to the extent of letting him drive for that other Stuttgart firm, Porsche. He took an eight-cylinder 908GTS on the Coupe des Alpes of 1964 where it persistently misfired on one of the wettest events in living memory. On the 1965 Monte Carlo he drove the homologated version of the same car, the 904GTS with the Finn, Pauli Toivonen as team mate in a similar car. Toivonen was one of the many who were overwhelmed by the fantastic blizzard of that year but Bohringer profited from his vast experience and got through. His drive in what was really a most unsuitable car for those conditions was as much a revelation as that of Timo Makinen in winning the rally outright. Bohringer proved that given an arduous task he could rise to the occasion despite his advancing years. He drove the low racing car, with its angled screen so prone to icing and with insufficient heating to keep it free even on the inside, as if he was back at the wheel of one of his comfortable Mercedes. He lost just four minutes on the road section and was third overall before the start of the final mountain circuit. Here he drove superbly to lose no further time on the road while the ultimate winner, Timo Makinen, lost four minutes with a broken distributor in his Mini-Cooper. Bohringer finished second overall in one of the

finest drives of his career and then shortly afterwards retired to his hotel in the forests near Stuttgart, a living legend.

The man who beat him on that epic Monte Carlo of 1965 carried on the legend-making of Carlsson and Bohringer. Timo Makinen is Scandinavian and very large; he is also a technician and perfectionist who can bring his talents to bear equally successfully on a sprint or an endurance event. His ebullient character and spectacular activities, both behind a steering wheel and away from it, have made him rallying's most popular character. He has not always been the most successful rally driver in that his list of victories is not as long as that of some others, but that can be attributed to the fact that he has not always driven a car capable of winning. Nevertheless, he has probably led more rallies than any man alive while his successes with the Mini-Cooper and with the Ford Escort are more than sufficient to show that he can win as well. At least twice in his career, he appears to have come to the point where he will be eclipsed by the rising tide of new rally stars, only to come back with an impressive display of his talents to correct such erroneous impressions. Time does not seem to have dimmed his ability to drive extremely fast, and he starts every rally amongst the favourites.

Timo's rallying started in 1960 with an apprenticeship in various Volvos and Saabs, with which he did ice racing and small but concentrated stage rallies which form the basis of motor sport in the Scandinavian countries. He had picked up his driving skills at the wheel of a newspaper delivery truck, working for his father. He seems totally unworried by the type of car he is given to drive, and has as much success with front-wheel drive cars as with the more conventional layout of front engine, rear-wheel drive.

His first supported drive was in a Mini-Cooper supplied by the BMC agent in Helsinki and in 1962 BMC brought him over to drive a Mini-Cooper on the RAC Rally as part of their effort to stop Erik Carlsson achieving his hat-trick of wins on that event. The attempt failed but Makinen did win his class and set some remarkable times on the stages, thus persuading BMC to take him into their official team for the following season.

The Monte Carlo saw him at the wheel of a Healey 3000, at that time the fastest rally car around, with the lady racing driver Christabel Carlisle as his co-driver. The Healey was not the best choice for the snow and ice of Monte Carlo's special stages while Miss Carlisle had never been on a rally before and Mr Makinen's command of the English language was still at a very basic level. Despite this, they won their class and gained BMC armfuls of publicity. Makinen had set his name on the list of rally drivers who can do the 'impossible' and created the legend of the Flying Finn.

There is actually no man to whom the term 'the Flying Finn' can be applied exclusively. Indeed, Rauno Aaltonen was one of the first Finnish drivers to leave his home country and participate with success in foreign rallies. It was his drives with a works Mercedes in 1961 that led to the first use of the term; since then, journalists have applied it to just about every Finn who ever jumped over a matchstick in a rally car. However, Makinen has done more than any other driver to deserve the title and in his role as a fast driver and a rumbustious ambassador for the sport he has become *the* Flying Finn to thousands of people all over the world.

His first season with BMC was not too successful and the ruggedness of the Healey 3000 was severely tested in his hands and often was not a match for the speed he demanded of it. The following year, the emphasis of the BMC team switched to the

Mini-Cooper S with the recognition of the new 1071cc engined model. It was Paddy Hopkirk who won the Monte Carlo with Makinen fourth but on the Tulip Rally he had his first outright win. He was suffering at the time from a frequent change of co-driver, whereas his team mates benefited from regular pairings with co-drivers who understood all their little foibles and could help them to realize their best performances, an essential ingredient for success on long-distance rallies. Hopkirk was at that time with Henry Liddon and Rauno Aaltonen with Tony Ambrose but Makinen just could not seem to find Mr Right. Then before the Tour de France of that year, his co-driver for the event, Don Barrow, fell ill and he took up at the very last moment with Paul Easter, previously a driver in his own right who had campaigned Mini-Coopers in rallies like the Acropolis. Easter turned out to be the catalyst that Makinen was looking for: a competent driver yet quiet and modest in all he did, the perfect complement to Makinen's extrovert personality. This crew had more than five years together when they competed all over the world and Makinen produced some of his most electrifying drives.

At the start of their first full season together, they won the 1965 Monte Carlo Rally with a 1275cc Mini-Cooper in conditions which forced over three quarters of the entry to retire. On the night that the rally had to traverse the Alpes Maritimes between Chambèry and Monaco, a freak snowstorm engulfed the area. Roads became virtually impassable and the last 100 or so competitors of the field of 260 were eliminated almost at once. With competition number 52, Makinen and Easter made the best use of the slightly better conditions at the head of the rally plus some very special ice racing tyres from Finland to be the only crew to complete this part of the rally without road

penalty. Despite losing four minutes on the road during the last night of the rally, Makinen came home a classic winner in the mighty Mini. Makinen and the Mini caught the imagination of the public. Sales of the Mini-Cooper in France shot up so fast that supply could not meet the demand while everywhere that he appeared, crowds pressed round to see the burly Finn and the little red and white car. 'Le Mini' had arrived in the biggest possible way and its originator, Alec Issigonis, frequently appeared at post-rally celebrations.

In Finland, where rally drivers are top sportsmen, Makinen was as well known as the President and continued to drive for the BMC agent in Helsinki, whose agency was in the name of Morris. Consequently, Makinen wanted all his rally cars to bear that insignia and when BMC arrived with an Austin-Cooper at the start of a rally, badge swapping had to be carried out before Makinen would drive it, although the cars were otherwise identical. In Finland's own major rally, the 1000 Lakes, Makinen always drove with his old friend Pekka Keski-talo, who knew the roads almost as well as Timo, and they won the rally three times in a row starting in 1965. The last time that he won with the Mini-Cooper an incident occurred that typifies Makinen's approach. Not long after the start of one of the longest special stages, the bonnet flew up on a jump, obscuring nearly all vision from inside the car. Pushing the tiny sliding window as far open as he could, Makinen peered at the road from a very strange angle and went on at almost undiminished speed to lose but a few seconds to his rival, Simo Lampinen in a Saab. Had he stopped, however briefly, to close the bonnet properly, he would have undoubtedly lost the rally, so small was his margin of victory.

When the Mini-Cooper era came to an end with the closing of BMC's competition department at Abingdon-on-Thames, Makinen spent a short time in a kind of limbo working out the rest of his contracted year with drives in privately owned cars. He led the RAC Rally of 1968 in a Clarke and Simpson Escort Twin Cam until the engine failed, while the following year, he took up with BMW for the Monte Carlo, and then drove a works Saab into fourth place on his beloved 1000 Lakes. Towards the end of 1969, he came to an agreement to do some rallies for Lancia and drove the front-wheel drive Fulvia on three major events for them. In the Tour de Corse, he drove an open prototype and managed to finish in this rather unsuitable car while on the Coupe des Alpes, the engine blew up. The final ignominy was to retire on the RAC Rally after hitting a stray dog on a special stage—the impact drove the Lancia insignia through the radiator.

The retirement on the Coupe des Alpes was his final attempt at an event in which he had never managed to crown his performance with success. In 1965, he had finished second to René Trautmann's Lancia Flavia Zagato, but since then the outright win had eluded him with such regularity that he never cancelled his hotel room in Marseille as he reckoned that he would be back there the first night. It was left to his team mate, Paddy Hopkirk to win that gruelling French classic for BMC in 1967 and in that same year Hopkirk netted another of Makinen's targets when he won the Acropolis Rally. Makinen had led the Acropolis several times with a Mini-Cooper but in the closing stages had found that his pace over the rough Greek roads was too much for the little car. On one famous occasion, the BMC mechanics had tipped his Mini onto its side to facilitate the changing of a drive-shaft when fuel dripped from a tank onto a hot exhaust and set the car afire. Makinen dived into the car while the mechanics

emptied the fire extinguishers from the service car onto the conflagration. They thought that he had risked his skin to reach the other extinguisher inside the rally car but instead he emerged, covered in smuts and foam, holding the passports and money wallet. Such exploits have made Makinen as well known for his failures as for his victories.

One rally which did elude him for many years but which has finally succumbed in the biggest possible way is the RAC Rally of Great Britain. He claims that it is his favourite event and considering that he said that long before he won it, he must now be very pleased with himself for he has won it three times in a row. He very nearly won it back in 1965, a year when ice and snow covered most of the route and made conditions far from ideal for his powerful, rear-wheel drive Healey 3000. Nevertheless, he got the big sports car into the lead ahead of Rauno Aaltonen in a Mini-Cooper but then a glassy ascent in North Wales brought him to a halt and the Mini skittered through to victory, albeit with a helping push. Since 1970, Makinen has been a works driver for the Ford Motor Company under his old BMC boss, Stuart Turner, and with the services of Henry Liddon as co-driver. He has won many events for them, especially in Finland where he has added one more 1000 Lakes win to his total and won the Arctic Rally on his way to becoming Finnish Rally Champion. For the RAC Rally of 1973, he was entered with start number 13 sponsored in his Escort by the Milk Marketing Board. Despite this, he came home a clear winner and has since repeated the performance twice, with different start numbers and sponsors.

The common characteristic of all great rally drivers is their self-confidence. A rally, especially one of the long distance events, is no place for a prima donna. During such an event,

The ability to win in conditions varying from desert dust to Arctic ice is essential in a successful rally driver. Timo Makinen seems able to win anywhere, in any type of car. Here, with Henry Liddon, he leads the 1975 Moroccan Rally (he later dropped back when the Peugeot 504 broke a drive shaft)

the driver must maintain a working rapport with the co-driver, the mechanics and the team manager in order to achieve the best possible result. He must thus have a great deal of self-control which can only spring from a degree of self-confidence. Scan the list of current rally drivers and you will find many who are quick enough to warrant a place in a works team but not so many who have achieved that distinction on a permanent basis. The reason is that driving talent is not enough on its own; it must be alloyed with sufficient self-confidence to overcome the varied situations that are part and parcel of rallying, and with sufficient modesty to make that confidence acceptable.

Also, to be a successful rally driver it is necessary to know quite a lot about the machine that is conveying you. Few drivers are fortunate enough to have such a strong car that they never have to think whether what they are handing out to it will ever break it. During a rally like the East African Safari or the Moroccan Rally, it is essential to keep consideration for the car very high on one's list of priorities, and familiarity with the car can help tremendously. No better example could be found than the 1975 Safari which was won by Ove Andersson in a works Peugeot 504. This talented Swede started out building his own rally cars from others that had been crashed, and his original Saab was a piebald example where the paint failed to cover the join between two halves of other cars. From a works drive with Saab, he tried his hand with Mini-Coopers before going to Lancia, and then having a magnificent season with Renault Alpine when he won four World Championship events including the Monte Carlo. He has also driven works cars for Ford, Peugeot and Toyota and now works for Toyota as team manager/developer/rally driver using his mechanical talents to their full advantage. On the Safari, he had a strong car but one which was completely outpaced by the works Stratos so he was forced to drive within the limits of the car and

wait for the Lancias to have trouble, which is exactly what did happen.

Rally drivers are a diverse lot and rules about their behaviour are hard to formulate. One cannot even say that one country produces better rally drivers than any other, although the nearest thing is the dominance of Scandinavian drivers over the last two decades of the sport. This must be attributed to the fact that rallying has been accepted as a national sport in those countries far more than in the rest of Europe where football is more popular. It is no surprise to find that there are few good cricket players in Finland where the game is not played, whereas that little country seems to give birth to a never-ending stream of highly competent rally drivers.

The most recent development has

been a re-emergence of really good French, Italian and German drivers, which has come about thanks to the interest of firms such as Renault, Citroen, Alpine, Lancia, Fiat, Alfa Romeo, Opel and BMW. Many of them employed established rally drivers, often Scandinavians, and matched their best native drivers in the team alongside them so that they could learn the techniques of modern rally driving. Now drivers like Jean-Luc Therier, Sandro Munari, Walter Rohrl and Achim Warmbold can show anyone the way home. The only country missing from this list is of course Britain. There are many top class rally drivers in Britain but the success of national rallies has meant that few of them have ventured forth to do rallies on the continent.

Presumably he gives it to his children, but it was strange to find Makinen endorsing milk on the 1973 RAC Rally *(right, top)*. Nowadays a driver can keep going for several miles on a flat tyre, secure in the knowledge that it will not become wrapped round the disc brake—Makinen on his way to his third RAC victory, in 1975 *(right)*.

A shower of champagne and then a chat with newsmen, preferably where TV cameras focus on the bonnet of the car so that the sponsor gets his message to a wide public, is an essential routine for victors. Makinen and Henry Liddon after their 1973 RAC win pose with Jack Kemsley between them

Driving

If you think about it, rally driving techniques should be far better catalogued than those of racing, for in every rally car there is a co-driver who can observe what the driver is doing and could subsequently record it for posterity. Perhaps it is the effect of being in a car driven by an apparent lunatic on a narrow mountain pass or a forest road lined with trees that renders the co-driver incapable of making objective records, but not much has filtered through to the general public about what a rally driver does to make his car go so fast. It is natural that if a rally driver has discovered a technique that gives him the edge over another driver in a similar car, he is not going to rush out and tell everyone. In the year of the Monte Carlo Rally when tyres were restricted, Timo Makinen kept his special studded tyres hidden in his hotel bedroom until the last minute and then drove down to the parc fermé with them. They were probably not significantly different to the tyres available from the Dunlop van but they had the studs fitted very carefully and he was convinced that they might just give him the edge on the other drivers. It certainly had an important psychological effect.

Despite a natural reluctance to divulge information which may help other drivers to beat them, rally drivers are like anyone else and love to show off their knowledge. People like Paddy Hopkirk and Rauno Aaltonen have taken part professionally in rally schools, while others show an increasing willingness to talk about their methods. Thus quite a lot is now known about their specialist driving techniques.

A good example with which to start is one of the slow-speed manoeuvres that is easy to understand: the handbrake turn. This consists of driving at a speed which should be at least 15–20mph, depending on the conditions, and then turning the steering

wheel and following it up immediately with a quick de-clutch and a sufficiently strong pull on the handbrake to lock the rear wheels. If all this is done correctly—and only practice will tell what is the correct co-ordination of movements—the car should turn through 180° in a road only slightly wider than its length. The end of the turn is effected by releasing the handbrake while correcting the steering and finally letting up the clutch to drive away in the opposite direction from which the car came. Anyone reading this and wishing to try it should start in a place where the road is a bit wider than the car's length or they may well leave their headlights on a wall.

This handy little trick was evolved in night rallying where it was regrettably sometimes necessary to turn the car round in a bit of a hurry after a navigational error. To take time out for a three-point turn would result in a certain penalty, but a quick alteration of the car's direction might just save the day. To finish with the technicalities of this stunt, it is best suited to front-wheel drive cars with the handbrake acting on the rear wheels, but it is pretty effective in a car with conventional layout of the engine up front driving the rear wheels. If the car is one of those front-wheel drive cars that has the handbrake operating on the front wheels, it is best to remember that in that case handbrake turns can only be done while proceeding in reverse, which is perhaps not quite so useful except in driving test meetings!

The handbrake turn can also be used in rallying to get a car round a tight corner. It is particularly useful on a loose or slippery surface where the car has a natural tendency to understeer, and has proved invaluable for negotiating hairpin junctions where the car would otherwise have to be shuffled round in a three- or five-point turn. The use of the hand-

Preceding pages: Per Eklund on his energetic way to fourth place in the 1975 Swedish Rally

brake is not as widespread as it was, the two things which have made it redundant being the discovery that a twin braking system can be set up to give a variable bias between front and rear brakes, and the adoption of the left foot for pushing the brake pedal.

It is best to deal with the twin brake system first as it will make the less conventional and more controversial left-foot braking easier to understand. Most people think that brakes are not the most important thing on a rally car and that provided they adequately stop the car in a straight line when required, then all is well. Very often a man will spend hundreds of pounds on his engine, gearbox and suspension without giving much thought to his rally car's brakes.

Competition pads and linings are a must and most people understand why. They are made from a very much harder and more durable material than ordinary linings and they can operate as a good friction surface at temperatures well in excess of those found in normal motoring. Anyone who has suffered from brake fade on standard linings will realise that when they get hot, the material starts to break down and will not grip the disc or drum. It is almost as if oil had been poured over them—no matter how hard the brake is pushed, the car just goes on and on. Competition pads will usually fade just once and then provide optimum friction even when the discs are glowing red hot. Thus rally drivers can be seen driving up and down a road near a service point where they have had new pads fitted, constantly applying the brakes to get them faded before they go out on the next special test. The best thing, of course, is to fade-in a few sets of pads before the rally starts and have them ready in the service car. This saves a lot of time and can be very important on a rally where there is no time to spend in addition to that taken for service.

The humble brake fluid is the next thing to be considered and this must have a boiling point sufficiently high to resist the temperatures found in the brake cylinders. It is no exaggeration to say that brakes run much hotter in rallying than in racing, for while there may be a few points on a race circuit where the brake temperature goes higher, in rallying the applications are more frequent and there is less speed to force cooling air round the brakes. The chances are that a lot of this heat will get transferred to the wheel cylinders and ultimately to the brake fluid. Everything possible is done to conduct the heat away and in this respect, the use of magnesium-alloy wheels has proved very successful. Because of their strength, such wheels can have much larger access holes for the cooling air, and in any case the alloy has a very good conductivity for heat and will take quite a lot away from the hub itself. There are differences in effectiveness between various types of alloy wheels, largely dependant on their physical design. One year Lancia found this out on the Monte Carlo when they used a new wheel and found that all their Fulvias were losing the brakes from the fluid overheating and boiling. The new wheels were quickly relegated to the rear of the cars and the old ones used on the front wheels, which cured the problem.

If all these things are right—the friction material, the brake fluid and the cooling of the brakes—then the rally driver has only tackled the easiest parts of setting up the braking system. The most important thing is to get the right balance between front and rear brakes, for in rally driving it is very rare that the driver can brake on exactly the right spot for each corner. He may get it right once in ten when he does not know what is coming, but that is a good score. Most of his braking will have to be done when he has been caught out, and would horrify any driving instructor. It may happen half-way through a corner because that corner tightens up or becomes a much sharper corner going in the other direction. If the surface was dry tarmac, the requirement would be to have a bigger proportion of the braking effect on the front wheels as the weight transfer under braking would put more of the car's weight over those wheels. However, if the car is already in the corner as described, because of the cornering forces generated by the tyres, one front wheel would have less weight on it than the other and would probably lock up and deprive the driver of half his steering forces. A similar problem will occur if the surface is loose or slippery when the front wheels will lock, even in a straight line, as there is not sufficient adhesion to transfer the weight to the front wheels. In both cases, the result is the same; the car will understeer off the road or at the very least become difficult to control.

Consequently, the rally driver prefers to have more braking effect upon the rear wheels than is considered normally acceptable. This is best achieved by splitting the front and rear brakes into different hydraulic circuits commanded by separate master cylinders. These can then be mounted close together and coupled mechanically by an adjustable bar on which the brake pedal acts directly so that the braking effect exerted by the foot can be divided proportionally between the two circuits. This kind of system is used on rally Fords and Opels and enables the driver to regulate his brakes so that he can have the optimum setting for a tarmac stage and then set them back for a loose surfaced stage.

With the bias of the brakes set to the rear, the car tends to perform a kind of de-tuned handbrake turn when the brakes are applied hard. This

oversteer effect is generally desirable for when a rally driver finds himself in a situation that calls for hard braking, to have the car already turning under the guidance of the brakes is a definite help. There is also the point that he is less likely to lock the front wheels, in which case he would lose what steering he had and worsen the situation. Most accidents that rally drivers have early in their careers are due to 'freezing on the brakes' with consequent loss of steering.

It does not even worry an experienced rally driver if he has to brake hard in a left-hand bend for a sharp right-hander. Because the car is already being steered to the left, it will swing more violently that way and the rear will slide out to the right. That may seem a bad preparation for a right-hand corner, but if in that situation the foot is lifted off the brake and the steering wheel turned to the right, the car will immediately rotate and point to the right with the rear of the car sliding out to the left. Just why it does this is hard to explain without going into a lot of applied mathematics about rotational and linear energy. Suffice it to say that it does but, like the handbrake turn, do not try it out in a confined space.

Most of what has been said about brake balance applies to all types of car no matter where the engine is located, although the weight of the engine does play a big part in the weight transfer that takes place under heavy braking. Front-wheel drive cars can present problems of their own and separate solutions have to be found. Consider a conventional car in the middle of a tightening corner. The driver applies the brakes and, because they have been correctly set with a bias towards the rear, the car slows and oversteers into the tightening part of the corner. He then applies power, the rear wheels spin a little and the car continues to oversteer through the rest of the corner. Had that been a

Great expectations of a 'mini-Porsche' followed the announcement of the Hillman Imp, but apart from Rosemary Smith's victory in the 1965 Tulip Rally, it never really made a mark. This is the works Imp of Tiny Lewis and Tim Bosence on the Monte Carlo in 1966

My, my, Ferdinand, how your beetle has grown. The unbiquitous VW lacked power for European rallying, but this example prepared by Porsche Salzburg had a 1600cc engine and a five-speed gearbox and was no sluggard. Photograph shows Gunther Janger and Dieter Gottlieb heading for second place overall in the 1972 Austrian Alpine

front-wheel drive car, the front wheels would have spun and not only would the oversteer effect have been lost but the car would have started to understeer as the front wheels lost their grip. It was to solve this problem that left-foot braking was developed.

It started in Finland with Rauno Aaltonen who is so much the theorist of modern rallying that he is dubbed 'the Professor' by many of the other drivers. He was driving a Saab 96 and discovered that it had this tendency to change from oversteer to understeer when the foot was lifted from the brake quite late in a corner and placed on the throttle. After some thought—and experiment—he decided that the left foot could be used for braking while he was still accelerating with the right foot; in other words the left foot was to control the rear wheels by means of the braking system while the right foot working in conjunction with the steering wheel controlled the front end of the car. The effect of applying the brakes was to make the car oversteer with the rear end coming round. An unexpected bonus was that the brakes also tended to inhibit either of the front wheels from spinning too much under the effect of power, and thus operated somewhat in the manner of a limited-slip differential. The technique caught on, especially through the successes of Simo Lampinen who also drove a Saab and learnt from Aaltonen, and Timo Makinen who applied it to the driving of the BMC Minis when he was in that team at the same time as Aaltonen. It was a particularly easy technique to use with a Saab as that car is fitted with a freewheel device which enables the driver to make clutchless gearchanges by just fractionally lifting his foot from the throttle and then moving the gear lever. Pauli Toivonen used left-foot braking in the ponderous Citroen DS19 and won the 1000 Lakes Rally in that car in 1961, as well as that scandalous

Monte Carlo Rally of 1966. Since then it has travelled widely and Sandro Munari perfected it with the Lancia Fulvia and won the Monte Carlo Rally for Italy in 1972. Of course, in those cars not possessing a freewheel device, the left foot has to be shifted to the clutch pedal for an instant in order to change gear, although anyone who has watched the driving sequence in the film *The Flying Finns* will have seen and heard Makinen changing without the use of the clutch.

Two things emerge from all this talk about brakes. The first is that there is an awful lot more to a simple thing like braking than could be imagined by anyone who has not been involved in international rallying. What setting should be used on snow and ice? Do racing tyres need a different setting to studded tyres? Should there be more or less rear braking under slippery conditions? These are questions which only experience can answer but at least one gets a glimpse of the complexity of the problems facing the rally driver. Secondly, left-foot braking is not much use as an everyday driving technique, but is a rally speciality for controlling a car in difficult conditions or a difficult car in more normal conditions. It has done a great deal to keep front-wheel drive cars in contention on international rallies far longer than they perhaps deserve. In ten years it contributed to five wins on the Monte Carlo Rally, and this did a lot to popularize front-wheel drive cars, which are now sold in larger quantities than ever before. While not wishing to deny that the front-wheel drive car is inherently more stable than other types, its rally results should be viewed with caution in view of the very specialist techniques needed to drive them that fast.

Before leaving the subject of left-foot braking, it should be mentioned that the brakes do get infernally hot as a result of being applied to guide the car as well as to slow it down. In the descent of an Alpine pass, the brakes get very little chance to recover by losing heat as the speed of the car is not high enough to supply a sufficient flow of fresh air. It is a common sight to see rally cars finishing a test on the Col du Turini during the final hectic night of the Monte Carlo Rally with their disc brakes glowing bright red or even orange. It may be spectacular but the driver has to be very careful not to keep his foot on the brake pedal while the car is stationary having its time recorded or else he is likely to boil the brake fluid or, worse, fuse the pads to the disc.

This technique has also been applied to cars other than those with front-wheel drive, although at present the number of drivers that have tried it is very small. It is alleged to give a further element of car control at high speed above and beyond what can be obtained by use of the steering wheel and throttle and as such seems to represent a step forward in driving technique. There is the additional advantage that with the left foot poised over the brake, the driver's reaction time is reduced as he no longer has to move the right foot from throttle pedal to brake pedal.

The driver who is best known for his left-foot braking in rear-wheel drive cars is the Finn, Markku Alen. He started using it on a Volvo 142 in Finnish rallies and has now used it successfully in Fords and Fiats. He feels that it gives him the chance to balance the weight of the car from front to rear and vice versa while tackling a long fast corner or sequence of corners. The Swedish driver, Ake Andersson, had the same idea and employed the technique when he was driving for Porsche in the late 1960s. The rear engine layout was more difficult to control in this way and, although he did win the Gulf London Rally in 1968, it was

probably instrumental in causing his crash on the 1000 Lakes a few weeks later.

Not all the developments in rally driving are directly concerned with driving technique—quite a few of them are technical improvements to the cars and components like lights, brakes and tyres. The best known of these must be the studded tyre. The search for something that would grip on snow and ice dates back to the time when rallyists first started their winter journeys to Monaco. This rally produced more ideas on non-skid attachments for car tyres than for any other single accessory. These varied from the familiar chains down to strips of canvas tied around the tread of the tyres. There were plenty of attempts to fix nails and screws into the tread of the tyre, but either centrifugal force threw them off or they penetrated into the inner tube and brought the car to an ignominious halt.

After the Second World War, technology came up with a carbide tipped screw that took much longer to wear out than mere steel, and fresh thought was given to practical ways of mounting these in tyres. The early ones were bolted to circular plates and passed right through the tread of the tyre with another plate on the inside to retain them. These were best known in the form fitted to Dunlop's famous Duraband radial tyre which dominated the rally scene for over a decade. Only a couple of dozen or so of these studs could be fitted to each tyre depending on its radius and width, but they made a big difference to the traction available on sheet ice or packed snow. In conditions of deep, soft snow, the clumsy chains were still most effective but no car could go very fast with them flailing around underneath it.

In Scandinavia, most motor racing takes place during the winter months, on ice tracks ploughed out on frozen lakes and rivers, and it was from this direction that the next improvement

was to come. The carbide tip of the stud was mounted in a steel or aluminium 'frame' which served as its holder. This meant that the amount of expensive carbide could be drastically reduced while the overall weight of the stud was also diminished. A hole was then drilled to a predeter-mined depth in the tread of the tyre and the frame shot into it under high pressure so that eventually just the carbide tip projected from the tyre. This technique did away with the heavy plates and meant that many more studs could be utilized in a single tyre. The flexibility of the tread

One of the definitive rally cars of the last decade has been the Renault Alpine. This is a 1600cc version, driven by Jean-Luc Therier and Marcel Callewaerts into second place in the 1971 Monte Carlo. Technical note is that

the white stripe on the tyre indicates a particular studding pattern for easy identification

was not seriously impaired while the amount of rubber allowed to touch the road in normal driving conditions was increased. The road holding of the tyre was better on snow and ice as well as on a dry road, where the stud acted rather like a cat's claw and retracted itself into the tread under the weight of the car. The pressure was sufficient to push it into snow or ice when required.

Tyres studded in this way can have anything from 150 to 750 studs, and the carbide tips can protrude from almost nothing up to 7mm. The longer the protrusion of the tip, the longer must be the frame to prevent the stud flexing too much in the tyre and this results in a heavier stud. When the tyre is rotating fast, there are considerable forces trying to pull the stud from the tread and sometimes the tread from the tyre. All the recent developments in winter rally tyres have centred around prevention of this eventuality. Pirelli retained the Swedish rally driver, Hakan Lindberg, to design and develop their range of rally tyres and in 1968 he came up with the MS35 which is still one of the most successful of loose surface and snow tyres. It is made in different rubber compounds, depending whether it needs to give its grip above or below freezing point, and also in a special one for studding. Its final development occurred when Lindberg designed a version especially for studding which had an additional layer of bracing above the conventional radial bracing. The holes drilled for the studs were allowed to penetrate this layer and when the studs were fired into the tyre by compressed air, a special flange on the base of the frame engaged behind the layer of bracing and made it practically impossible to pull out the stud. It was a great improvement as tyres which have been driven hard either lose their studs or the poor things waggle around like rotten teeth. It was on Pirellis with the extra bracing that Sandro Munari won the Monte Carlo Rally in 1972 and he would be the first to give them some credit for his exceptional performance that year.

Some pretty unbelievable tyres have made their appearance in rallying and none more so than the Rengasala used by Timo Makinen to win the very snowy Monte Carlo Rally of 1965. The tyres were re-moulds and had about six hundred pieces of metal resembling penknife blades moulded into the tread. Each blade projected out from the rubber about 10mm and was not made from carbide but ordinary steel. These tyres were originally produced for ice racing when the ice was covered by fresh snow, and were excellent in penetrating the soft snow produced by the Alpine blizzards that engulfed the 1965 Monte Carlo. To go to the other extreme, studded tyres have also made their appearance on the East African Safari where the only snow to be found is on the tops of Mounts Kenya and Kilimanjaro. It was discovered that they gave better traction in the soft mud that forms on African roads when it rains. The red murram soil becomes unbelievably sticky and clings to the tread of the tyre so effectively that adhesion is reduced to zero. The studs help to break up the layer of mud adhering to the tyre and reach through it to grip the road. The only catch with using them is that you have to stop and put them on and then take them off again after the muddy section. That requires a lot of pre-planning to have the tyres and mechanics at the right place, and a lot of time is lost through the double tyre change.

While talking about the Safari, it would be difficult to find another rally where 'know-how' counts so much towards success. A muddy road in Africa can have less traction than a skating rink and few of the European driving techniques can be used in such a condition. The overseas drivers found this out the hard way and it is one reason why they took so long to produce a Safari winner. The local drivers say that the murram roads have a high crown in the centre and, while it is desirable to stay on that, the overgrown parts of the road at each side are equally good to drive on. It is just a case of knowing that there is unlikely to be any obstruction and then driving flat out through grass as high as the car. Thus, if there is a muddy section with cars stuck in the middle of the road, a European might slow down and try to thread his way through, but a local would take to the sides with no significant reduction of speed.

On most rallies, if the car stops for any reason, the crew are well aware that they are gathering penalties. The Safari is no exception in that respect, but it has to be realized that there are occasions when it is necessary to stop and perhaps do a survey on foot before driving through a difficult obstacle like a flooded river. Most cars carry hand winches so that if they do get stuck, the winch cable is strung between a convenient tree and the car which is then slowly cranked out. The local inhabitants often help with a pull in return for money and one has to know that they are bright enough not to pull on a steel hawser which will cut their fingers, so a useful addition to the kit is a hempen rope. High-lift jacks working on a simple hydraulic principle are carried so that a car can be raised out of ruts and then pushed sideways off the jack so that it lands clear of them. On one famous occasion, the great Carlsson was stuck in ruts on the Mbulu section so he and co-driver, Gunnar Palm, rolled the Saab onto its roof and then back onto its wheels a comfortable distance from its original resting place. Because the Saab is nicely rounded it rolls without suffering much damage, and very few people who saw the car at the finish could believe the story. To convince the sceptics, the Swedish pair, still wearing dinner jackets, went outside the prize presentation and repeated the stunt.

Rally driving is very much a question of being well prepared for an event. A driver can only go as fast as his talent and experience will allow, but there is much greater opportunity for a man whose anticipation behind the steering wheel is matched by his anticipation of other problems. Not many rally cars carry spare parts unless they are unlikely to see any service cars for long periods. The idea is to carry the minimum amount of weight in the car and no one wants to weigh it down with spare gearboxes and springs when they can be carried around in a service car. It is a good idea, however, to know what is likely to prove fragile on the car and carry just the right spares to get it going in the event of those parts breaking. Rauno Aaltonen once did a rally for BMW in a 3·0 litre coupe and he happened to know from his experience of racing these cars that the distributor drive shaft was a weak point when the engine was being revved to its limit. Thus he decided to carry a spare distributor complete with shaft. Sure enough, the thing broke right in the middle of a stage but, having done his preparation correctly, he was able to change it on the side of the road and carry on in the rally.

All the fast driving and preparation can go for nothing if details are overlooked. Something as simple as changing a punctured tyre can turn into a disaster if the crew are unfamiliar with the use of the tools and have not practised wheel changing as a co-ordinated activity. There is a world of difference between changing a wheel on a firm surface in broad daylight and doing it on a loose surface in the middle of the night with other cars rushing past and showering dirt over the operation. With crash helmets on, the crew have difficulty in hearing even shouted instructions and they must know before they start who is going to do what. It is no good doing the job and jumping back into the car only to discover after ten miles that the jack and wheelbrace are still on the side of the road.

It is impossible to finish this chapter on rally driving without mentioning pace notes. This is a fascinating subject and would easily justify a whole book, for there is an aura of mystery about them which make them a compulsive subject for discussion whenever people are talking rallies. The curious thing about these funny symbols is that they were introduced to the sport by a racing driver, Stirling Moss. He used written shorthand notes to describe roads when he drove the Mille Miglia—and won it—with Denis Jenkinson in 1955. They were using a Mercedes Benz 300SLR and the Germans evidently took up the idea, for the Mercedes team dominated the results of the 1960 Monte Carlo Rally by doing a careful recce and noting down the bends so that they could be read back to the driver during the rally proper. In the late 1950s, British teams such as BMC and Rootes were entering crews in rallies like the Acropolis, the Liege, the Coupe des Alpes, the Tulip and the Monte Carlo where it was possible to recce the route beforehand. They started sending out one team member to make navigational notes plus detailed comments on how difficult each section would be during the rally. Tony Ambrose and the late John Gott were the boffins behind many BMC successes, while Norman Garrard performed the same task at Rootes. Gradually danger spots such as bumps and bad bends found their way into the navigation notes, and it was only a short step from that to making a complete record of all the bends on a speed test in the manner of Mr Moss. Tony Ambrose was the first to try this when he did the Acropolis Rally for BMC and it caught on very quickly. The early notes soon evolved into modern pace notes which give a shorthand word picture of the bends plus the stretches of straight roads between them. There is no standard notation for the bends along the lines of Mr Pitman's excel-

A moment of panic for the eventual winners of the 1969 Monte Carlo Rally, Bjorn Waldegaard and (visible) Lars Helmer. In the confusion at the service point, Waldegaard mistook the instruction 'nicht bremsen' (don't brake) for the opposite, and the rear pistons popped out of the calipers. This cost four minutes in road penalties . . . but not the rally

Perhaps you have to possess an inverted sense of humour to be a Saab driver, but Finns certainly possess an intense national pride. This Scan-Auto Saab Finland entry for Tapio Rainio and Klaus Lehto in the 1974 RAC Rally was painted in the national colours of blue and white

lent shorthand; each driver has his own idea of how to grade bends and this is reflected in the words he uses. In any case, a Frenchman would be unlikely to make much of notes written in Finnish!

Paces notes used on rallies today are very sophisticated and will give a driver almost as much information about a road as he could usefully remember by driving over it dozens of times. The limiting factor to the amount of information is often the time it takes the co-driver to read it all out. In this respect, the English language has proved its usefulness in brevity of expression and very often two Swedes will use English in preference to their own language solely for pace notes. This question of how long it takes to read out the information becomes doubly important when what are called 'ice notes' are employed on a very important rally

like the Monte Carlo. In this case, the team will have experienced crews passing over the stages shortly before the rally and marking parts of the road which are icy or snowy or dry on a copy of the pace notes that competitors are going to use. If something goes wrong and the ice note crews do not get back to the start in time to hand over the annotated copies, they use the originals and play the ice and snow as it comes. However, these ice notes crews play a big part in the rally for it is on the information supplied by them that the crews choose which tyres to fit at the start of the stage. If there is a lot of snow and ice, then heavily studded tyres must be used, while if it is dry they may choose racing tyres. Of course there can be an in-between condition or the conditions may be changing, which brings us back to luck, skill and experience once again.

Almost Standard

An oft-quoted benefit of motor sport is that it provides a test bed for developing cars and their ancilliary parts. In this context, the example of the disc brake is best known as Dunlop and Jaguar made much of it in connection with their victories in the Le Mans race. The competitive nature of sport forces drivers to extend their cars to the limit and any improvement which the designers can give them can immediately show in results. Rallying during the post-war years has been a more important source of development than racing as the cars used in modern racing bear little resemblance to normal road going cars. This problem extends to an extent into rallying, for as its prestige increases, cars built by the manufacturers for rallying begin to resemble more and more their relatives on the race tracks rather than those on the public roads.

This was not always the case. In the pre-1914 era, people used to build cars, either at the factory or in their own workshops, which were specially designed to tackle a particular event. In those days there were very few regulations concerning the cars; frankly, there were very few cars and many manufacturers so that a system of regulations governing the cars had hardly had time to come into existence. Each event had a list of things which could or could not be done and provided that the cars complied with those, the modifications carried out had no limit.

Even local laws were sometimes waived in favour of a visiting driver who would, nowadays, be able to look up such things in the international laws governing the sport. In racing, the situation was 'internationalized' much earlier due to the existence of major international races such as the Gordon Bennett series and the very wide public interest shown during the early part of this century in the Land Speed Record.

It took at least another two decades before there was any concept of international laws in rallying. That did not mean that there were no rules about which to argue, for each event had its own set and they grew more and more complex in an effort to try and make the rally a more equal contest. So many different varieties of car existed, that the drafting of rules to fit them all was a hard task. The production line system of producing cars which Henry Ford had devized with such success in the USA was not widely adopted in Europe, where cars tended to be made on a 'one-off' basis for particular customers.

One of the most successful men in this field was Ferdinand Porsche who worked for the Daimler factory in his native Austria in the pre-1914 era. He designed, built and drove the winning Daimler in the 1910 Prinz Heinrich Fahrt. This car had overhead valves and separate steel cylinders of 105mm bore and 165mm stroke. It gave almost double the output of the normal Daimler and, with its contoured body, would exceed 90mph with relative ease at a time when the outright Land Speed Record stood at 127mph, credited to a Stanley Steamer. These special Austro-Daimlers swept the board in the rally and the three cars entered by the factory filled first three places overall. So elated were the factory that they announced their intention of selling the 'Prinz Heinrich Daimler' as a standard model in a similar fashion to which the Ford Motor Company sold their 'Escort Mexico' after a prototype push-rod Escort won the London to Mexico Rally in 1970. One would have thought that the Edwardians would have seized upon this superb example of rallying improving the breed, but, not for the last time, Herr Porsche found himself ahead of public taste. Few people bought the Daimler as it was evidently too fast and went round corners at speeds that were

Preceding pages: a local spectator shows little interest in an Alfetta GT in the 1975 Acropolis Rally

dangerous to the human constitution. Porsche stayed on with Daimler for almost another ten years, incorporating his ideas in existing models rather than designing completely new ones.

The First World War had a very significant effect upon motorized transport. Military historians may still argue as to whether or not the appearance of tanks on the Somme was the turning point of the land battle, but the period saw the emergence of incredible developments in the use of cars, lorries, motor cycles and buses. Consequently, technical development was forced along at a pace unequalled in peacetime. As soon as the High Command realized that the internal combustion engine vehicles had many advantages over horse drawn equipment, then the whole resources of Britain and her Allies were put to making more and more vehicles of better and better performance. During 1916, the USA produced more than a million cars for the first time in a single year, while by 1923 Ford alone was producing more than two million in twelve months.

In 1922, the Austin Seven made its appearance in Great Britain and the joys of motoring could be had for a mere £225. Such cars as Ford's model T revolutionized our way of life in the third and fourth decades of this century, although they did not make an immediate impact on motor sport. This was still the privilege of the hand-made sports car and the powerful saloon but at least the Model T owners were showing interest in what was going on. Herbert Austin realized this and started racing with a sports version of his top selling Seven. One could hardly say that these Austins looked just like the car you could buy but they were far closer to it than the majority of cars racing at the time.

The Monte Carlo Rally of 1924 was won by Jean Ledure in a 2-litre Bignan saloon which though coming from a small factory, was pretty much a typical example of a normal saloon. Lurking under its bonnet was a production engine, modified only in its duplicate wiring circuit in case the demands of its four headlamps and three windscreen wipers proved too much for the standard circuitry. Two years later, the Hon. Victor Bruce won the event with an AC Tourer complete with a hood and a single extra spotlamp fitted to the driver's windscreen pillar. With such cars, the public could identify more easily and could imagine without too much difficulty that they too could win a major rally. The exploits of such gentlemen as Malcolm Campbell and Henry Segrave could only be emulated in their wildest dreams.

The victory of the AC was not typical, for the late 1920s saw more victories going to large saloon cars, although Jean Bignan won the Monte Carlo of 1928 with a Fiat having just 990cc while Hector Petit won in 1930 with a 904cc Licorne. Between those two years, Dr Sprenger van Eijk won the Monte Carlo with a 4·7 litre Graham Paige while in 1931, Donald Healey won with a 4·6 litre Invicta sports car. Evidently, the reliability of the big engined cars made them more suitable for long distance events and they gradually did much better than the small cars, unless the handicap imposed by the organizers went too hard against them. In the shorter but more difficult rallies involving steep and twisty work in the Alps, the lighter cars came off best. The precursor of the modern Skoda, the Laurin and Klement, had a very good record in the Alpenfahrt where its light weight proved a help when the heavier cars found that their brakes were totally inadequate for sustained downhill work.

During the 1930s, there were a host of names to juggle with in rallying, Fraser Nash, Delahaye, Jaguar, Hotchkiss, Bugatti, Renault, Talbot,

Triumph and Fiat among them. Gradually, the successful rally car began to evolve away from the saloon car as rally organizers began to rely more and more on speed and outright performance to decide the winner. The Liege-Rome-Liege was first held in 1931 and this soon set new standards. The average speeds demanded of competitors in the Alps and Dolomites made sure that only powerful cars stood any sort of chance for overall victory. The smaller cars could always try for a class win or the index of performance, but light sports cars with big engines became the most popular rally cars. Of course, this was not true for all rallies and the Monte Carlo in particular continued to be dominated by saloon cars, not all of which had big engines. This was for two reasons: firstly, the wintry conditions likely to be found on the route were far more bearable in a saloon car with its associated creature comforts and secondly, the driving test on the promenade came to dominate the results with the road section meaning less and less as tyres and winter driving in general became more proficient.

A sight guaranteed not to please the French! Donald Healey with his 4½ litre Invicta and trophies after winning the 1931 Monte Carlo Rally. He set the fastest time on the only special stage, the Mont des Mules hill climb

A sight guaranteed to please the French, even though Louis Chiron did not drive a French car to victory in the 1952 Monte Carlo. At least his Lancia Aurelia was made not far away, in Turin. One imagines that the wings were sprayed a light colour to reflect light forward from the car's headlamps

Following pages: the increasing popularity of rallying has meant that the number of hazards on special stages increases in direct proportion to spectators' cars. The additional spotlights on the Aaltonen and Easter Datsun 240Z in the 1971 Monte are aircraft landing lights

Outrageous cars appeared, such as the special bodied Ford of Colonel Berlescu with a superstructure made entirely of canvas and wood. The idea was to lower its weight and centre of gravity for the all-important driving test. That same year, 1936, the rally was won by a similar Ford but with a little more standard bodywork comprising the front half of a production Ford with cut-away doors and no rear end to speak of. These freaks led to some serious thinking amongst the Monte Carlo organizers. Whatever else one may say about those august gentlemen, they have never been slow to formulate a regulation and try by doing so to advance the sport. Their efforts have sometimes backfired but

their deliberations on this occasion resulted in a regulation that called for competing cars to be standard saloons or drop-head coupes utilising normal production chassis. Furthermore, superchargers were banned and the general ambience of the rule was to accept only cars of a very much more standard type that had previously been accepted.

The direct result of this was that in the post-war years, a need arose for some kind of definition of a standard or production car and the international organization of the FIA devised a recognition form that manufacturers had to complete if they wanted one of their cars to be accepted as in regular production. Thus the infamous

A Ford won the 1964 East African Safari but it was not this Lincoln Mercury Comet (*above, left*), one of eight entered by Ford of America, although two of the massive American cars did finish and won their class. The Datsun stuck in the background was one of the first Cedrics entered by the factory. At the half-way point of the 1973 Safari, Clark and Porter (*left*) were leading but after the re-start mechanical trouble put them out. Seconds count at Safari controls – Philip Hechel (*above*) realises as he runs to the clock that any delay may mean that another car will pass them at the re-fuel point and then their Peugeot 504, driven by Hugh Lionnet, will have to run in the other car's dust for hours. Special lights for special conditions as seen on the Aaltonen-Easter Datsun 240Z on the 1973 Safari (*right*). The large horizontal flaps are intended to prevent much mud being splashed onto the main lights; in any case the high-mounted light will stay clean

homologation form was born, on which the basic details of the production car were listed along with the numbers in which it had been, or was about to be, produced. This was a very serious attempt to make rallying the proving ground for Mr Average's Automobile and most other rallies followed the example of the Monte Carlo Rally. There were exceptions and when the Liege-Rome-Liege and the Coupe de Alpes were revived after the 1939–1945 war, they threw open their doors to anything that had four wheels and could pass scrutiny as a motor car. So sure were the organizers that their events were the pinnacle of toughness that they were prepared to let drivers have a go with anything. This acceptance of prototypes for road events lasted until 1964 for the Liege when it was held for the last time and until 1969 for the Coupe des Alpes for when that rally was held for the last time in 1971, it was open only to recognized cars, properly homologated.

Hotchkiss won the first two Monte Carlo Rallies of the post-war era, one with a pre-war car, one with a virtually identical model. On the Coupe des Alpes, limited production sports cars won most of the prizes and typical were Leslie Potter in an Allard and Donald Healey in a car of his own design and manufacture. This was soon to change, for in 1948 Jaguar announced their XK120 six-cylinder, twin-cam sports car and the supremacy of the standard sports car was established. Ian Appleyard won one of the only two Golden Coupes ever awarded, by winning individual Coupes for unpenalized runs in 1950, 1951 and 1952. The car that he used was that immortal XK120, NUB 120, which has been seen by enthusiasts all over Britain at exhibitions. Other XK owners were no less successful and bandleader Johnny Claes became the only man to ever finish the Liege-Rome-Liege without road penalities

when he won that event with a XK120 in 1951. Such sports cars ruled the roost in rallying and if the XK was Britain's contribution to the scene, one should not forget the Lancia Aurelia GT, an example of which won the Monte Carlo Rally of 1952 with Louis Chiron at the wheel.

As usual, the catalyst for change was the Monte Carlo, which was not only one of the best known rallies but was also held first in any year so that its fashions tended to be copied by events that came later in the season. The Monte Carlo organizers contrived to make things more difficult for the GT cars by applying a handicap to the results. This built up gradually until in 1966 there was the ridiculous situation where the GT cars staggered along under a 20 per cent handicap and it was the revulsion from this that finally brought about the modern situation where the Monte Carlo is run on a scratch basis. It was significant, however, that an event like the East African Safari—at that time called the Coronation Safari—which was held for the first time in 1953, only accepted absolutely standard cars on which no modifications of any kind were allowed. That rule was finally rescinded in 1960 but the rules continued to favour the standard saloon car until it was accepted into the World Championship on the late 1960s. Indeed, a sports car did not win it until 1971 when Edgar Herrmann and Hans Schuller won with a Datsun 240Z.

The saloon versus GT battle really got under way in those immediate post-war years and to some extent is still raging today. On the loose surfaced special stage rallies of northern Europe or the long distance events in Africa, the saloon cars get the better of their GT rivals, while on tarmac rallies the situation is reversed. The reasons for this reversal are many, but basically a saloon car has more sus-

This beautiful piece of the roadmaker's art is called the Vivione, and is one of the most difficult sections in the Dolomites. The car is the works Sunbeam of Sheila van Damm and Ann Hall, and the event is the 1954 Alpine Rally

A big sports saloon in the tradition of earlier Monte Carlo winners was this Jaguar Mk VII that Ronnie Adams drove to victory in 1956, ably assisted by Frank Biggar and Derek Johnstone

This car may have Colt written on it but it is actually Hannu Mikkola's winning Ford Escort in the 1000 Lakes Rally in 1974 — Colt in Finland is a cigarette firm who sponsor Mikkola's rally efforts. (*right, top*) Roger Clark's hair will remain smart for his sponsor is Cossack, the hair-dressing for men — a tie-up which has done much to promote rallying

Evidently a man who likes to keep abreast of the news even when he is going sideways is Russell Brookes (*right*) whose sponsorship in 1975 came partly from *The Birmingham Post*. The rest came from Andrews Heat for Hire, who rent out industrial heating equipment, and Brookes turned out to be a real hot-shot, ready to oust Clark from top position in British rallying

Left: in Morocco, Jean Deschaseaux and Jacques Plassard are legends of the desert—they know it so well that they can take one of their famed short cuts and pop up in front of you like a mirage. They gave the Citroen SM its only major competition victory in the Moroccan Rally of 1971, but they were less fortunate with this DS21 in 1973.

Below: another patch of problems in the Dolomites is the Gavia where Rauno Aaltonen's attempt to win the 1963 Liege-Sofia-Liege finished up against the iron rail. Here a Renault 4CV tackles the Gavia ten years earlier

Colin Malkin (*left*, on the Scottish) tried hard but never really got the Chrysler Avenger GT among the Escorts. Sensation of 1974 was Markku Alen who was 3rd in an Escort on the 1973 RAC Rally after lying 177th at one point. Fiat took him into the big-time. Here (*right*) he struggles with the 124 Abarth Spyder on the 1975 Swedish Rally

Left, top: the idea of advertising is to get a message over, but on this Renault 12 Gordini there seems to be message saturation. The driver runs under the pseudonym of 'Le Tahitien' but presumably he did not engage Gaugin to paint his car for the Moroccan Rally

Left, lower: away from Europe, works drivers often drive locally-prepared vehicles. Pat Moss and Liz Nystrom drove several times for the Renault importer in South Africa and here they tackle the 1970 Total Rally in a 16TS

Above: Finland in August can be a Super Place but it can rain as well as the competitors in the 1973 1000 Lakes found out. Veteran boatman, Timo Makinen won in an Escort while Markku Alen in this Volvo 142S was second

pension movement available and is more 'chuckable' than a GT car which has a more refined handling based on a low centre of gravity.

After the Second World War, saloon cars became decidely more sporty in an attempt to provide the family motorist with pleasure that had previously been reserved for the young batchelor and his intended. The Sunbeam Talbot and Jaguar saloons were immensely popular and both had sports car derivatives in the Alpine and the XK series which used basic-ally similar suspension, engines and gearboxes as the bread-and-butter saloons. The sports cars distinguished themselves on rallies like the Coupe des Alpes with Stirling Moss emulat-ing Ian Appleyard's achievement by winning a Golden Coupe with his Sunbeam performances in 1952, 1953 and 1954, although it must be admit-

ted that his 1952 Coupe was achieved with a 90 saloon from which the Alpine was later derived. On the Monte Carlo Rally, saloons still held their own with Jaguar winning it outright with Ronnie Adams in a Mark VII in 1956, the same gentleman help-ing with the marque's team victory in that rally during 1953. For Sunbeam, their saloons had an envi-able record in the team prize on the Monte Carlo and this culminated in a win for their 90 saloon in the hands of the two Norwegian policemen, Per Malling and Gunnar Fadum in 1955. Sunbeam went on to produce their Rapier Saloon which was a successful rally car, even well into the 1960s.

One should not imagine that the post-war rallies were easy affairs. It is true that the average speeds set would be easy to achieve with modern cars, but now we are used

109

to finding events like the Monte Carlo taking place on tarmac surfaces. In those earlier days the roads in the Alpes Maritimes, or the Dolomites on the Liege were often loose surfaced and a rally car received a pretty good hammering no matter what event it did. The cars did not have such specialized suspensions as are now commonplace, nor did they have a wide range of tyres to choose from. Studded tyres were in their infancy and radials were only a whisper gleaned from some unwary development engineer. The creature comforts in the cars were much less than in a modern car and while Ian Appleyard might well put the XK's hood down on a daylight section of the RAC Rally (then held in March), or Sheila van Damm tackle the Dolomites in summer with an open Sunbeam Alpine, the night section of a rally like the Liege-Rome-Liege could produce cockpit conditions best described by reference to the traditional brass monkey. The late John Gott used to drive his Frazer Nash open to the Alpine breezes and he was by no means alone in his taste for fresh air, but one should remember that there were no powerful heaters for keeping windscreens demisted and most drivers preferred the improved visibility that folding the windscreen flat provided. Few modern rally cars have tried that solution since modern lighting systems have made night into day with the discovery of the halogen (iodine vapour) bulb. Matra Simca did use open versions of their prototype sports car to win the Tour de France, while Chrysler France have also been responsible for the little open 2-litre Simca CG that Bernard Fiorentino campaigned in French rallies in the beginning of the 1970s. Lancia too have used a cut-open version of their Fulvia Coupe for rallies like the Tour de Corse. It was called the F & M Special after Cesare Fiorio and Claudio Maglioli who developed it,

but was unpopular with the drivers who had to dress up as if they were going scuba diving.

Towards the end of the 1950s, there· was a definite change in rally cars that went beyond any fashion or attempt to beat rules. Mercedes had brought full scale professionalism to rallying and had made a business of winning rallies. They employed their crews on a full time basis, sent them out to reconnoitre the route where possible, tried to find the right tyres for tests that needed something special and supported the rally cars with crews of mechanics and fully equipped service cars. The established teams of Rootes, BMC, Ford, Renault, DKW and Citroen were not slow to see that they too could do these things and took up the Mercedes challenge, although it was not without some carping about professionalism pushing the sportsmanship aside. On one infamous occasion, Walter Schock pulled out of the RAC Rally when his nearest rival in the European Championship had retired, for that meant that he had won the title and did not need to drive any further. That was not an action that endeared him to his fellow competitors.

All this had an immediate effect on rally cars. They started to sprout more lights and, with the influx of Scandinavian drivers into the works teams, roof lights which could be swivelled by the co-driver became all the rage. The cars had to be fitted with improved electrical systems to cope with the lights and other extras such as heaters, demisters, twin-speed windscreen wipers and an increasing collection of navigational instruments. For the first time, the alternator seemed to be the only device capable of supplying all this power and it is largely due to rallying that so many modern cars are fitted with them today. Heating and demisting in postwar cars was nothing to write home about and even when the Mini was introduced at the end of the 1950s, its heater was so poor that drivers often asked 'What heater?' when it was referred to in conversation. Again, the influence of rallying has produced proper devices for modern cars.

Perhaps the biggest changes in cars came about thanks to the lack of conservatism of continental car manufacturers. Citroen had no qualms about front-wheel drive, nor did they hesitate to put their air/liquid suspension onto a production car. The ID 19 and its later deratives was a most successful rally car and one of its earliest wins was with Paul Coltelloni on the Monte Carlo Rally of 1959. Eleven years later, the big Citroen was still lively enough to lead the London to Mexico World Cup Rally at Lisbon after the European sections, although sadly that event was to see the death in an accident of Ido Marang who had driven with Coltelloni in the early days. In the interim, drivers like the late Lucien Bianchi, René Trautmann, Olivier Gendebien and latterly, Jean-Claude Ogier, gave the Citroen many victories as well as many stirring drives in rallies like the Liege-Sofia-Liege and the Safari where success just eluded them.

With the commercial success of the Volkswagen in Germany, others were bound to copy it and Renault jumped on the bandwagon with their fabulous little 4CV which also had its engine over the back wheels. This car was not only successful in its own right but it was to be the springboard for the development of two even more successful Renault rally cars. At its first attempt at the Monte Carlo it finished fourth overall and also won the Coupe des Dames, a performance which made Jean Rédele decide to build a fibreglass sports car on the 4CV chassis. Rédele had himself been a rally driver under Francois Landon for Regie Renault and his Alpine A106 was very much designed with such events in mind. This was harking back

to the specials of the 1930s but Rédele was able, through his connections with Renault and his own astuteness, to build up his business to the point where he had sufficient production to get the car recognized under the modern rules. The A110 derivative from that early car became the most successful rally car of the late 1960s and it was only in the mid-1970s that it was finally forced out of competition by the new minimum weight regulations.

The other derivative from the 4CV was to be the Renault 1093 which was originally projected as a competition version of the 4CV by none other than Amédée Gordini. By the time the project got going, Renault had brought out the Dauphine and Ondine range and so the competition model was based on that chassis rather than the original. Despite its title, the 1093 did not have an engine of greater than one litre but had a tuned 850cc engine mated to a five-speed gearbox. Jacques Feret, who was later to succeed Landon as Renault competitions boss, drove one to victory in the 1958 Monte Carlo Rally and this was to be the last time that a Frenchman in a French car won that classic until 1973 when Jean-Claude Andruet won it with a Renault Alpine A110.

Both these spheres of Renault activity were to establish precedents for the rest of the rally world. It was the first time that a major manufacturer had taken one of his standard products and developed it and sold it with such non-standard parts as a five-speed gearbox and a ready-tuned engine. It was also the first time that someone in the post-war era had taken on the supply of standard parts to a smaller firm to enable them to build a completely different car especially for competition. Firms like BMC, Ford and finally Fiat were to follow suit and this was to completely change rally cars during the next fifteen years.

More than
Standard

A modern rally car can be picked out at a glance from more mundane runabouts. The sump guard, wide wheels, large bore exhaust, spotlights and square yards of advertising material will identify it immediately, and probably draw a crowd of admirers if it is parked in a public place. Frequently these same admirers will apply the external trimmings to their own cars to give them the look of a rally car; often they succeed. However, most of the money spent on preparing a rally car goes on those things which cannot be seen—inside the engine, the transmission and the suspension. Looking back, one tends to think that the rally cars of earlier times were less prepared for the rallies that they had to tackle, merely because they did not have the external appearance of today's highly modified cars. Unless they were off to Monte Carlo, when the car might well be covered in shovels, chains and spare wheels, only the rally plates front and rear would give the game away. Spotlights, for instance, were few and far between and the most common extra fitting was a small swivel light for reading signposts.

The fact that rally cars went virtually incognito was founded in the reluctance of many manufacturers to get officially involved with the rally teams using their cars. Citroen never sanctioned the entries made by René Cotton in the name of the private team, Paris Ilê de France, but all the cars had consecutive registration numbers and were followed by service cars from the factory. When Lancia started rallying in the 1960s, Cesare Fiorio obtained permission to borrow the cars and mechanics, but no work was allowed to be done within the walls of the factory and the cars had to be entered by HF Squadra Corse, the sporting side of a club run for people who had owned Lancias for more than a certain number of years. Their emblem was the elephant that had adorned the last Lancia Formula One car, and has now become famous throughout the rally world.

The British and Germans became more directly involved and ran factory teams. BMC, Rootes, Mercedes and DKW were prepared to accept failure as part of the struggle for victory, and ran their operations out in the open (although the spirit of amateurism was strong even within those teams). Rallying might well have stayed like this for ever had it not been for the arrival on its scene of a small Swedish aircraft manufacturer with just a single works car.

The professionalism of Mercedes had made people realize that there was much that they could do behind the scenes with their cars and drivers to help to win major rallies. Even the works teams used to go into major events to 'drive blind', using maps and instinct, but after Mercedes showed what could be done in the way of pre-rally recces, the idea caught on in a big way. The BMC team started to use detailed pace notes to read back the road and thus enable their drivers to go faster. These notes were Tony Ambrose's brainchild but soon other teams saw the advantage they gave and adopted them into their repertoire. The Renault and Citroen teams had realized very early on that a competent service network could help to resist failure even if it could not guarantee victory. Their Monte Carlo wins in 1958 and 1959 were in no small part due to superior groundwork.

But it was Saab that put the whole show together—recceing, pace notes, preparation, service—and did it in such a way that Erik Carlsson won the Monte Carlo twice in a row, not to mention many other outright wins. Saab still set a high standard of organization today, which is part of the benefit of being a small outfit and Swedish. At the same time that Carlsson was making his impact on

Preceding pages: 1965 RAC Rally loser (Timo Makinen's Austin-Healey 3000) and winner (Rauno Aaltonen, Mini-Cooper)

Hunchback the Volvo PV544 may have been, but it had a better track record than Richard III. Both it and its predecessor the PV444 had many successes in rallying and Gunnar Andersson, photographed here on the 1962 Monte Carlo Rally, won the European Rally Championship in 1963 before retiring to become Volvo's competition manager

the rally world, the Swedish Volvo team, although less publicized, was not far behind them. Gunnar Andersson won the European Championship for them in 1963 while Tom Trana collected that award in 1964 and won the RAC Rally in both years. Indeed among British enthusiasts, his hunchbacked Volvo PV 544 was as popular as Carlsson's Saab. All this success and the reasons behind it did not go unnoticed and the man on whom they had the greatest effect was a bespectacled English co-driver who in 1960 had been with Carlsson and in 1961 inherited the post of BMC competitions manager from Marcus Chambers. His name of course was Stuart Turner and in his five years at BMC, their team became the greatest force world rallying had then seen.

The Austin-Healey had been a mainstay of the team for many years and had won many rallies. In its final six-cylinder, triple Weber, aluminium headed version as the Healey 3000, it was by far the most powerful rally car, with well over 200bhp at the fly-

wheel. Hans Walter occasionally used a Porsche Carrera 356 with a 2-litre, four-cam engine which gave somewhere near that figure, but otherwise the Healey 3000 was in a class of its own. It was unwieldy and not all its drivers felt at home behind the steering wheel. The exceptions were Timo Makinen who twice finished second on the RAC Rally with such a car, and Don Morley who with his non-identical twin brother, Erle, made a speciality of winning the Coupe des Alpes. Anyone meeting the Morley brothers for the first time could have been forgiven for thinking that tall Erle was the driver, but in fact it was the diminutive Don who could manage the big car with such ease. Only an axle failure in 1963 prevented the Morleys from joining the select band of drivers who have gained golden Coupes.

Strong and long-legged, the Healey was the ideal long-distance car even if it did not provide much in the way of creature comforts for its crew. It won the Liege-Sofia-Liege twice, with Pat Moss in 1960 and with Rauno

Aaltonen in 1964, but the changes in rallying started to leave it behind. No longer was the ability to accelerate as important as that of negotiating corners at speed—pace notes and special stages had made sure of that. By 1966, the competition programme of BMC was centred on a small box with 10-inch diameter wheels, which bore not a single resemblance to an Austin-Healey except in the retention of the name Austin.

The Mini first appeared in 1959 and at first was ignored by BMC, who were then rallying the MGA Twin Cam and the Healey 100-Six. In comparison with these, the little box did not seem to be a real car at all. With its 850cc engine, it was distinctly underpowered.

Its first competition sorties were in the hands of BMC's lady drivers, Tish Ozanne and Nancy Mitchell. The sight of Saab winning rallies with an 850cc front-wheel drive car of considerably greater weight prompted further evaluation and by the Geneva Rally of 1960, it was going well enough for the Morley twins to beat Mr Carlsson. On rougher events it was less suc-

cessful and attempts at rallies like the Acropolis and the RAC met with failure. In September of 1961, the Mini-Cooper was announced—the fruit of co-operation between John Cooper and Alec Issigonis—and with its 997cc A series engine, disc brakes and wider wheels, it was a real super-Mini. Turner joined BMC a month later and almost his first decision was to put some of these new cars into the next Monte Carlo Rally where Pat Moss won the Coupe des Dames, although classified 'only' 26th overall. She did much better on the Tulip Rally a short time later when she won it outright and gave the Mini-Cooper its first international victory.

BMC lost Pat Moss to Ford at the end of 1962, but by then Turner had acquired the three 'Abingdon Musketeers', Timo Makinen, Rauno Aaltonen and Paddy Hopkirk, who were to take the Mini on to its greatest competition successes. If it was a rally winner in 997cc form, then greater things were expected when in 1963 the first 'S' type was announced. This boasted a 1071cc engine giving 70bhp in standard form, larger disc brakes and wider $4\frac{1}{2}$J wheels. Within weeks of its announcement, it had won the Coupe des Alpes with Aaltonen and terminated the Tour de France a remarkable third overall and first in handicap with Hopkirk. It proved fragile on the RAC Rally where Hopkirk survived to finish fourth overall but for the Monte Carlo Rally of 1964, it was a sensation. It beat the new Ford Falcons—Ford America had thought victory was theirs for the taking—as well as all the established teams of Saab, Mercedes and Volvo to give Paddy Hopkirk a win that was to establish both him and the Mini-Cooper as the new heroes of rallying.

Within a year, the 1071cc engine had become 1275cc and with something like 110bhp on tap, the Mini-Cooper started to clean up in all sorts of rallies. Volvo might still win in Sweden and Lancia in Italy, but elsewhere the mobile box began to make an impression not only in the tarmac events which suited it so well but also in quite rough rallies. Its Moulton rubber suspension was a factor which aided it greatly, but one factor that counted against it was its small wheel size. Much development was put into making it strong and, by 1965, Aaltonen was able to win many of the tough rallies behind the Iron Curtain, which together with a brilliant win on the RAC Rally at the end of the year was sufficient to confirm him as European Rally Champion. Makinen had won the Monte that year and gone on to start a hat-trick of victories on the 1000 Lakes, so the Mini-Cooper had shown that it could win almost anything and everything. It was amazing in its versatility and, thanks to the tyre-wisdom of the Finns, it could be adapted to rallies on tarmac, ice, snow, sand, rock and gravel, and always go quicker than the opposition. It flew the British flag in rallies and races all over the world and through 1966 and 1967 kept the forces of Ford, Lancia and Porsche at bay in European rallying. In some ways, its last season was perhaps its best, for under the direction of Peter Browning (who had replaced Turner), Hopkirk won both the Coupe des Alpes and Acropolis rallies, which had previously eluded him, while Aaltonen won the Monte Carlo and Makinen the 1000 Lakes. The Mini was not officially withdrawn from competition because it had become uncompetitive, but rather because of internal politics and economics within British Leyland, as BMC had then become. In 1968, experiments were going on with 1500cc engines running on fuel injection, not to mention other things tried out in the field such as 12-inch wheels and more powerful limited-slip differentials. The signs are that, with continuing development, the Mini-

Cooper could have kept at the forefront of rallying for many years more. As it was, the last works car to be built was constructed in 1970 and its last result was to finish second overall on the Scottish Rally of that year, driven by the evergreen Hopkirk.

In rather the same way that the Saab had evolved from the two-cylinder, two-stroke 92 through the very successful three-cylinder, two-stroke 96 to the present day four-stroke V4, the Mini had progressed from 850cc through two other capacities to 1275cc, winning rallies as it went. Both these cars helped to popularise front-wheel drive at a time when most cars had their engines well separated from the driving wheels. It was their competition success that has made so many of Europe's car manufacturers turn to front-wheel drive for their production models. The car which to some extent took over where they left off also had front-wheel drive and its career saw several upratings of its engine capacity.

The Lancia Fulvia was first seen on rallies in 1965 when Leo Cella won the Italian Rallye dei Fiori with a saloon version of this front-wheel drive car. On the Monte Carlo Rally of 1966, he finished fifth with a similar car behind the Lancia Flavia Coupes of René Trautmann and Ove Andersson. Until this moment, the Flavia had been the most successful of the Lancias, winning the Coupe des Alpes in its Zagato version with Trautmann in 1965. But now on that same Monte Carlo, the Coupe version of the Fulvia made its debut driven by the Finn, Jorma Lusenius. It was powered by the same 1100cc engine as the saloon but its superior handling and power-to-weight ratio made it much more competitive than the saloon. Cella gave it its first victory in the Rallye dei Fiori of 1966, which was very popular with the factory as the narrow angle V4 engine was much more in the Lancia tradition than the

The present-day Lancia team with their smart Alitalia uniforms and highly-painted cars originated from humbler beginnings. The early cars, like this Flavia Coupe, were borrowed from the factory and their only identifying mark was the 'High Fidelity' sticker featuring the little elephants. Despite the possible associations of Turin with Hannibal and his elephants, the animals came from the original mascot on the Lancia Formula One car

One of the most remarkable performances in recent times was the double victory in 1969 and 1970 of Harry Kallstrom and Gunnar Haggbom on the RAC Rally in a Lancia Fulvia Coupe (*centre*). Until then, the little car had been very much the bridesmaid to the more powerful Fords, Porsches and Alpines, but suitably encouraged Lancia went on with it to win the 1972 Monte Carlo (Munari during that event, *lower*) and Moroccan rallies

flat four unit of the Flavia.

During the remainder of 1966, success eluded the little coupe even though Andersson nearly came through to win the RAC Rally with one, and only mechanical failure kept him back in seventh place. With a bigger team, more money and more Scandinavian drivers, the Lancia team tackled 1967 with a 1300cc engine and almost as much power as the Mini-Cooper. Although their car was heavier than their rival, they made up for it by choosing a very low final drive ratio which gave them a top speed of only some 80mph. Unlike more conventional team managers, Cesare Fiorio was prepared to try anything from his technical box of tricks to give his drivers the best chance of winning and nothing was too impossible to try. Lancia drivers recall with horror his eight-speed gearbox which was the normal four-speed gearbox allied to a two-speed gearbox, which Fiorio got past the scrutineers as a 'mechanical overdrive'. Wrestling with a steering wheel, three pedals and one gearlever is enough for most rally drivers and the addition of another gearlever was not popular. Most of the team breathed a sigh of relief when a five-speed gearbox was homologated towards the end of the year! Other Fiorio ideas were more successful. The best example was the tyre change in the middle of a tight road section on the 1969 San Remo Rally which was completed in less than a minute and sent the works Lancias off on a critical special stage with brand new studded tyres. Not surprisingly the Fulvias finished the rally one-two-three.

Back in 1967 they had a harder fight. Ove Andersson started the year by nearly winning the Monte Carlo Rally in which the cars were limited to eight tyres on which to do all the stages. He finished eleven seconds behind Aaltonen's winning Mini-Cooper and beat Vic Elford's Porsche 911S, causing the first recount in years. He was second on the Acropolis and won the Spanish Rally while Lancia's new Italian sensation, Sandro Munari, came second on the Geneva Rally and then won the Tour de Corse in one of the most brilliant drives of his career. He was so fast that he nearly became the first man to ever finish that rally without penalisation on the road sections. Despite so much potential, 1968 saw Lancia in the doldrums despite Pat Moss winning the Coupe des Dames on the Monte Carlo and taking second place on the San Remo while new boy, Hannu Mikkola, was second in the Austrian Alpine. Munari missed nearly the whole year thanks to a terrible accident on the concentration run of the Monte Carlo Rally and when he was again fit to drive at the beginning of 1969, the Fulvia Coupe was already sporting its new 1600cc engine. It was not homologated in time for Monte Carlo where Harry Kallstrom won the controversial Rallye Mediterranée for prototypes with it, but Munari was soon cleaning up the Italian rallies and he went on to win the national championship. Kallstrom did even better and won the San Remo Rally, the Spanish Rally and the RAC Rally, as well as finishing high enough in other European rallies to clinch the title of European Rally Champion.

With the Fulvia now going so well, Lancia expanded their participation in rallies and tried just about everything, including the Safari to which they were to become regular visitors. Kallstrom won the RAC Rally again for them and Simo Lampinen topped the lists in Portugal but in other rallies, they found that the competition was starting to outpower them. Just when the Fulvia coupe was about to be pensioned off as both a production and competition car, Munari won the Monte Carlo with it. This most famous of Italian victories was the springboard that enabled Fiorio to expand his competition department even more and go on to build the Stratos. The Fulvia continued in production but only in its 1600cc coupe form and after Munari had used it alongside the Stratos to win the European Rally Championship in 1973, it was dropped from the competition programme and replaced by the Beta coupe.

Frankly, there seems to be a limit to the amount of power that can be applied to the road through the front wheels of a car. Towards the end of its rally life, the Fulvia was giving in excess of 160bhp and needed more and more powerful limited-slip differentials to prevent excessive wheel spin which consequently made the car more difficult to drive. The Beta is another front-wheel drive car, and it started off with a 2-litre engine giving some 200bhp which gave problems of traction. In order to make it competitive on loose surfaces, a lot of experiments were carried out with larger diameter wheels, detuned engines and power steering to overcome the effects on a driver's arms of a powerful limited-slip differential.

With rear-wheel drive, there is less problem with transferring power to the road and there were plenty of people making cars like that! The leaders were Ford, who, apart from the Taunus 17M, had not produced a front-wheel drive car and firmly believed that the engine should be under the bonnet and the axle under the boot. Their competitions department got under way in the 1950s when Zephyrs, Zodiacs and Anglias were prepared in the workshops of Lincoln Cars at Brentford in Middlesex. Big victories eluded them in Europe, for it was back in 1953 that Maurice Gatsonides had won the Monte Carlo in a Zephyr, and it was in rallies like the East African Safari where Ford regularly carried off the

team prizes and class wins that the company had most success. The new Anglia in 997cc overhead valve form showed promise but it did not have enough power or handling to put it right at the top. On British rallies where it was used with larger engines of up to 1500cc, it was supreme and showed to good effect on rallies like the Liege-Sofia-Liege which allowed prototypes, but it was the coming of the Cortina and its 1600GT derivative that really put Ford on the rallying map.

The Cortina GT first appeared in 1963 with Henry Taylor just losing the Touring Category on the Coupe des Alpes to Aaltonen's new 1275cc Cooper S. That same year, Peter Hughes and Billy Young finished second on the East African Safari with a 997cc Anglia, and in 1964 they headed a Cortina landslide in that event, defeating Carlsson's Saab in the process. Vic Elford took the Cortina GT to first place in the Coupe des Alpes and went on to finish third on the RAC Rally while in 1965, a quietly spoken gentleman called Roger Clark won the Scottish Rally with one. The Cortina GT was a good handling, well braked car but it lacked power, even from the twin Weber version of the 1600cc push-rod engine. There was, however, a Lotus Cortina with a Twin Cam engine developed by Lotus which was capable of giving much more power. This car was very successful in races and Vic Elford and David Seigle-Morris had won the handicap section of the Tour de France with such a car in 1964, but its A-frame, coil spring rear suspension was considered too fragile for rallying.

At just this moment, Henry Taylor stopped driving and became Ford's rally manager. He asked himself two questions: was it possible to build the Lotus Cortina with the rugged leaf spring rear end of the Cortina GT and, if so, could Ford make enough to get

Following pages: 'here come the Yanks' may have been a rallying call on the banks of the Potomac, but in 1963 it only raised slight curiosity amongst the rally world when they were told that Ford of America was going to enter a team of Falcon Futura Sprints on the Monte Carlo. Surprise of the rally was that one of them crewed by the Swedes, Bo Ljungfeldt and Gunnar Haggbom, set fastest time on *all* the special stages and would have been right in line for a win had they not lost considerable time changing a clutch on the road sections

Above: although Roger Clark has been British champion four times, abroad his luck has varied more widely. However in 1968, the first year of the Escort, he won both the Acropolis (pictured here) and the Tulip Rallies

Left: worth all the travelling—a works Escort, crewed by Hannu Mikkola and Jim Porter, won the marathon 1972 Heatway Rally in New Zealand in convincing style

Below: after 13 years, a Britisher won a British rally when in 1972 Roger Clark and Tony Mason came first in this fuel-injected Ford Escort

the car homologated? The answer to both questions was 'yes' and the new car's debut as a Group 1 vehicle was the controversial 1966 Monte Carlo Rally. Roger Clark came fourth overall but was then disqualified, along with the Mini-Cooper drivers for an alleged lighting fault. Ford's star of the year was Swede, Bengt Soderstrom who won both the Acropolis and RAC Rallies with the Lotus Cortina, which proved an excellent loose surface rally car though not quite able to match the Mini-Cooper S on tarmac. Part of the problem was that the Cortina was relatively high-geared and also it took Ford a bit too long to realize that it was possible to use racing tyres in a rally situation.

A Mark 2 Lotus Cortina came out in 1967 and while both Clark and Soderstrom won rallies with it, Ford's heart was not in this car. They had something else to concentrate on in the shape of a new car known in the factory as 'Brenda' but launched in the wider world as the Escort. It was an Anglia replacement and was smaller and lighter than the Cortina, but the top of the range model was a Twin Cam powered by just the same engine that had been used in the Lotus Cortina. This was now giving over 170bhp and the new car was evidently going to be ultra-competitive. Ove Andersson placed one third in its first-ever competition appearance on the San Remo Rally, and within weeks, Roger Clark drove one to win the Circuit of Ireland. He went on to win the Tulip, Scottish and Acropolis rallies, while Soderstrom also won the Austrian Alpine with the new car. The Escort Twin Cam also brought to an end the run of Makinen/Mini-Cooper wins in the 1000 Lakes when a youngster called Hannu Mikkola, who had cut his teeth in the Lancia team, was loaned a Ford and won the Finnish classic with ease. Even Makinen got in on the act and drove a privately prepared Twin Cam

on the RAC Rally that year and led until the engine failed. Ford were at that time concentrating their efforts on the London to Mexico World Cup Rally, which Mikkola won for them at the wheel of a push-rod 1852cc Escort (a 'Mexico' variant of the Escort was later marketed).

The Twin Cam was not capable of staying with the new breed of Porsches and Renault Alpines, but there was already a new Escort variant on the stocks. Stuart Turner had come out of his 'rest period' at Castrol and Ford's engineers were planning on fitting a 16-valve head to the Twin Cam block to make the RS 1600. The clever dodge was that it was homologated at 1601cc which meant that it could have its engine bored out to the limit of the class, which was two litres. Consequent development has seen the engine go through 1760cc and 1852cc versions and more recently to 1998cc with the adoption of an aluminium block. Makinen joined Ford shortly after Turner and the team was set for a renewed onslaught on the rally scene.

The Twin Cam finished fifth overall and best Touring Car on the Monte Carlo Rally of 1970 (driven by Clark), while the following year Mikkola led the East African Safari until the cylinder head gasket blew. Great things were expected of the new engine with its increased power and torque. Unfortunately, Renault Alpine had just got their 1600cc, 1800lb plastic peril to perform reliably and in 1971, the first year of the RS 1600, Ove Andersson took the French car to four outright wins in major rallies, including the Monte Carlo. The Ford was successful on the majority of British events but the RAC Rally was a snowy affair and Mikkola did well to finish fourth just ahead of Makinen while Clark, less at home than the Finns, finished eleventh.

A different sun shone on Ford's efforts in 1972, for Jean-Francois Piot

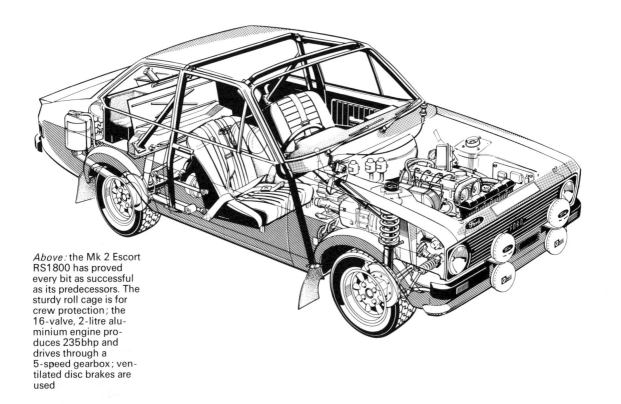

Above: the Mk 2 Escort RS1800 has proved every bit as successful as its predecessors. The sturdy roll cage is for crew protection; the 16-valve, 2-litre aluminium engine produces 235bhp and drives through a 5-speed gearbox; ventilated disc brakes are used

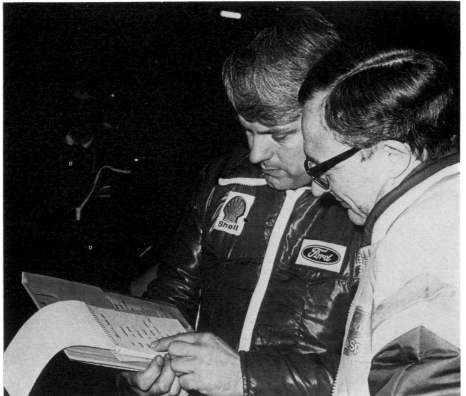

Left: Svengali and his Trilby—Stuart Turner (without hat) with Roger Clark at the start of the 1976 Monte Carlo Rally

Right, top: sophistication of the Escort continues in the cockpit. On this Mk 1 version, the switch below steering wheel (with wire attached) is a master electrical switch which can also be operated from outside the car

Right, lower: with the Escort, it is important to transfer weight from the front to the rear to increase traction and improve handling. Thus the spare wheel, fuel tank, oil reservoir, petrol pumps and battery are located in the boot

started by winning the Touring Category of the Monte Carlo Rally and then Mikkola made a place for himself in rally history by becoming the first European driver to win the East African Safari. The previous year Ford had used the Twin Cam, thinking that the dusty roads of Africa would lead to trouble with the exposed rubber camshaft belts of the RS engine, but in 1972 they put aside their doubts and Mikkola vindicated their trust. He

also won the Scottish Rally in a fantastic duel with Clark and the British driver responded by going ahead and winning the RAC Rally, the first British driver to do so in thirteen years. He was also supreme in the British national championship, winning it by a large margin.

Since then, the Escort RS 1600 has proved its worth in many rallies and nowhere more so on the RAC Rally where Makinen, a man who seems

This is what sideways driving is all about as Roger Clark and Jim Porter oversteer through a right-hand corner on a forest special stage. The spectators will have learned not to stand so close for car number 2!

to like hat tricks, won it for three years running following Clark's victory in 1972. He has also won the 1000 Lakes with it, as did Hannu Mikkola in 1974 before leaving to drive for Fiat. The Escort has proved its value as a long-distance car as well as a good sprint car on loose surfaced rallies but, thanks to the development of specialized rear and mid-engined cars, it has not been able to show capably good results from rallies like Monte Carlo. Thus Ford started a development programme to make the car more competitive on tarmac, which saw its fruits in rallies towards the end of 1975. Theorectically, a car like an Alpine or a Stratos must be at an advantage on a rally which uses mountain roads, but neither Ford's engineers nor their drivers are yet convinced and their efforts to prove their point will make rallying more interesting in the years to come.

Special Breed

In the previous two chapters, one can see that the popularity of rally cars has oscillated between the sports car and the saloon. Basically, purists insist that rallies should be reserved for normal road cars as they take place principally on normal roads, not on specially prepared tracks. However, there have always been events that have encouraged the use of racing cars and prototypes. The Tour de France is one that springs immediately to mind, although it is not a 'pure' rally by any means, involving the use of as many race circuits as rally stages. As strongly as the purists have supported the use of saloon cars and what one might call standard sports and GT

Preceding pages:
Therier extending his
Alpine in dusty Greece

Below: Elford at Turini. David Stone looks apprehensively out of Vic Elford's works Porsche on the 1967 Monte Carlo. Leaders until the last few stages, this snowfall dropped them down to third overall behind the front-wheel drive cars of Rauno Aaltonen and Ove Andersson

cars, the manufacturers of Europe have turned more and more often to what would have previously been called prototypes in order to keep ahead in the race for rally car supremacy. It all started back in 1967 prior to which the victories of the Mini-Cooper, Mercedes, Saab, Volvo, Sunbeam and even Austin-Healey had all

given the purists much joy.

Apart from being famous for the exclusion of the winning Mini-Coopers, the 1966 Monte Carlo Rally also saw the 'defeat' of Gunther Klass in a Porsche 911. He was defeated not so much by his fellow competitors but by the handicap system which was grossly unfair to GT cars. He set

several very fast times and would normally have finished well up in the results, but the handicap pushed him out of the top twenty. Porsche were naturally dissatisfied and looked into the problem to see what they could do about it. They discovered that their 911 had sufficiently large internal dimensions to qualify as a saloon car and since they made it in sufficient numbers to be recognized, they went ahead and homologated it as such with the CSI. The version that was recognized started to wipe up touring car races and, more important, Vic Elford and Pauli Toivonen were signed up by Porsche and run as the official rally team. Elford had a great year, starting off with a third overall on the Monte Carlo Rally and then

winning the Lyon-Charbonnieres, the Tulip Rally and the Geneva Rally—all championship events. The following year, Toivonen finished second behind Elford's winning Porsche on the Monte Carlo and then went on to win five other European Championship rallies and the title. The Porsche did not stay as a homologated Touring Car for long and by the time Bjorn Waldegaard came to win the Monte Carlo twice running and complete his hat-trick on the Swedish Rally, it was already back in the GT category, but the point had been made and few rallies were run on a handicap basis any more.

Rally organizers had woken up to the fact that no one liked handicaps and that, given a fair chance, the GT

The Renault Alpine came out of a long period of development to win literally dozens of rallies in the 1970s. This photograph shows Jean-Pierre Nicolas and Michel Vial during the 1973 Austrian Alpine which was provisionally won by their teamate, Bernard Darniche, but after protest and counter-protest was won by Achim Warmbold's BMW 2002

The gendarme may well look puzzled as to how this device got let loose on the road. The occasion is the 1972 Tour de Corse when prototypes were allowed for the last time and the subject is the Simca CG open version powered by the two-litre Chrysler engine. Brave pilot is Bernard Fiorentino while the even braver co-driver advancing with the time card is Maurice Gelin. They finished second overall

Less successful than the Simca CG, the Ford GT70 was a project which captured the imagination. The idea was to build a rally winning GT car from lots of standard bits but it suffered every imaginable setback and lacked reliability. Guy Chasseuil, who persevered with the car in many French rallies, on the 1972 Tour de Corse

This car went on to win the Tour de France, but on pure rallies as shown here in Corsica it was less successful — the JS 2 Ligier, driven by Jean Ragnotti. The car and its Maserati engine would undoubtedly have been a greater success in rallying had the owner of the project not had his sights more firmly set on Le Mans and the Formula One scene

cars and saloon cars could mix it on reasonably equal terms without any form of artificial levelling. The success of the Porsche was indisputable and yet it could never quite make out on rallies like the Safari and the RAC Rally. Its only true rival in Europe, was the Alpine Renault which after a long period of development and evolution emerged to win most of the classic rallies in the early 1970s with Ove Andersson heading a list of talented drivers with wins on the Monte Carlo, the Austrian Alpine, the Acropolis and the San Remo Rally in 1971. In 1972, Alpine Renault finally achieved the result they most wanted, when they won the Monte Carlo Rally with an all-French crew of Jean-Claude Andruet and Mlle 'Biche'.

In view of such successes with cars which ranged near the upper limits of the established GT world, other manufacturers could scarcely afford to turn the other cheek. Even such a conservative firm as Saab produced the Sonnet, which used the basic mechanicals of their successful saloon clothed in a fibreglass disguise. In truth, it was not much lighter than the saloon and although it appeared in the hands of Simo Lampinen on the Monte Carlo, when it was disqualified for missing a passage control, it never caught on and Saab went back to their saloons. Chrysler dabbled with a project using a sports car from the small factory of Charles Deutch, which was given various engines until success was obtained with the power unit used in the Chrysler 180 and the whole thing was called the Simca CG. It was never homologated as only a handful were produced but it had quite a lot of success in French rallies in the hands of Bernard Fiorentino who frequently beat the Alpine works team. At one time there was talk of making it a Chrysler Europe project with a view to producing it for sale, but this was destined to go on the pile of discarded ideas. The Ford Motor Company, however, dabbled with the idea of a racing-rally car in more depth despite the fact that their Escort Twin Cam—later to be the Escort RS 1600 with 16 valve engine—was already a very successful rally car.

No sports car had ever rolled off a Ford production line, for the GT40 was strictly an outside project financed by Ford. The idea was to design a car which, like the Alpine, was made up of a large number of standard components built onto another chassis with a fibreglass shell. Brakes from Zodiacs, struts from Cortinas and engines from Escorts were amongst the parts of the original concept but even with the genius of ace-designer Len Bailey, the project ran into problems. It was soon clear that the GT70 was going to have problems meeting all the requirements of the European traffic authorities so that it could be sold as a production car, while as far as competition was concerned it needed too large a proportion of non-standard parts to make it competitively reliable. A rally programme run in conjunction with Ford France spluttered along, showing excellent promise but few results, and eventually with the collapse of the production possibility the project was dropped and Ford went back to winning rallies with their Escorts.

Less hampered by restrictions on the sort of cars that they can build, the Italians have always been at the front of the exotic car market. Lancia had been rallying their front-wheel drive Fulvia Coupe since 1966 with numerous increases in engine size from 1100cc right up to 1600cc. This little car, though technically a GT car, had more in common with saloons, Harry Kallstrom winning the European Championship with it in 1969, the RAC Rally in 1969 and 1970 and finally the Monte Carlo Rally in 1972 with Sandro Munari. However, the

The man who has done more than anyone to shape rallying in the last decade—Cesare Fiorio of Lancia. Starting out as a driver himself with a Lancia Flaminia, he was among the first of the continental team managers to employ Scandinavians en masse. He also encouraged Italian drivers and his faith in Sandro Munari has been rewarded many times over, especially since the advent of the Stratos which was his brainchild. Among the very few ambitions that he has not yet realised is a win on the Safari, but that is not likely to elude him for long

competition life of the Fulvia Coupe was nearing its end for it was outpowered by Escorts, Opels, Porsches and Alpines; even the Fiat 124 Spyder was soon to outdo it. Lancia had to find a new rally winner and their competition boss, Cesare Fiorio, had just the thing up his sleeve.

At the 1970 Turin Motor Show, Bertone had exhibited a car based on a Fulvia chassis in the special bodywork section. This striking GT car had the Fulvia engine and gearbox subframe at the rear rather than in its normal position. Fiorio fell in love with the design and immediately approached the Lancia management with his idea—to build a Stratos. It was evident that the 1600cc twincam engine of the Fulvia would not

be powerful enough to make the car a Porsche-eater so he obtained permission from Piero Gobbato, the Fiat director in charge of Lancia at that time, to approach Ferrari for the use of their Dino engine and gearbox unit. Gobbato had previously been in charge of Ferrari, which was another branch of the enormous Fiat empire, and soon Fiorio had his engines. There was some talk at this time of using the 2-litre Abarth engine as Abarth was not only in Turin but was also part of Fiat, but that company's involvement with the Fiat 124 Spyder project rather ruled them out. In any case, Fiorio had his connections with Modena and he even ran the Ferrari pit at the Targa Florio in 1972 when Munari won the race with Arturo Merzario in a works Ferrari.

The Stratos was unveiled at the 1971 Turin Show and although a lot of people at that time thought that it was just an attempt by Lancia to break into the exotic GT market, it soon became clear that this was to be a serious challenger for the World Rally Championship. Throughout 1972, tests were done at Lancia's own track at Chivasso, on mountain roads in France and finally on dirt roads in Italy to develop the Stratos and get it ready for its rally debut. This was in the Tour of Corsica, when Munari retired with a broken rear upright (at that time was a fabricated part rather than a cast one). Despite the fact that the car was not yet homologated and could thus only be entered in events which would accept prototypes, Lancia pressed on and gained as much experience as possible in hill climbs, races and, of course, rallies. In 1973, Munari won the Firestone Rally in Spain with a Stratos and launched himself on a year that was to see him become European Rally Champion. Many of his other results were obtained with the Fulvia Coupe, but he drove a Stratos in the Targa Florio and would have won but for a broken seal which dropped him to second place. He won the Tour de France in fine style but failed to repeat that success on the Giro d'Italia when the four-valve per cylinder engine let him down.

December 1973 saw another major step in the Stratos story for Mike Parkes, after many years as a successful race driver and engineer for Ferrari, joined the Lancia team as a consultant engineer to help develop the Stratos and the Beta Coupe. One of his first tasks was to try a Turbo version of the Stratos engine and to try to iron out the bugs in the four-valve cylinder head engine. There was no immediate success with these two projects for although a Stratos won the Targa Florio in the hands of Gerard Larrousse and Jean-Claude Andruet it was powered by a two-valve engine, and Munari retired the car with the four-valve version. It was something of the same story on the Tour de France when Munari retired in the Turbo Stratos while leading, while Andruet went on to finish third overall behind two Ligiers powered by Maserati engines. These French cars could well have become a force in rallying had they been developed along the right lines but their owner was aiming towards the ultimate prototype, Formula 1, and left rallying alone. On the other hand, Lancia were seeking to produce sufficient Stratos to get the car homologated so that they could press on with their World Championship plans.

All through 1974, Munari campaigned the car in Italy, where rally organizers accepted prototypes and the result was that it gained a great deal in strength and its performance on loose surfaced roads became as good as it was on tarmac. On October 1st, the Stratos was recognized as a Group 4 production GT car by the CSI and within a matter of days Munari had won the San Remo Rally, a World Championship round. Within the month, he had won another round at the Rideau Lakes in Canada, but on the Press-on-Regardless Rally in the USA the alternator failed. Meanwhile, Andruet had won the Giro d'Italia with a Turbo Stratos and then went on to win the Tour de Corse with a more normal car. Munari took a Stratos on the RAC Rally and confirmed his own brilliance and the basic superiority of the car by finishing third overall in a most restrained drive to ensure that Lancia had enough points to clinch the World Championship title.

In 1975, Lancia's aim was the same—to become World Champion. But first they had to settle some internal politics for they were competing directly against the Fiat team and since all the money was coming from the pocket of Sig. Agnelli, there had to be some rationalization of effort. Lancia started by winning the Monte Carlo with Munari ahead of two Fiats driven by Hannu Mikkola and Markku Alèn and within two weeks had added the Swedish Rally with newcomer Bjorn Waldegaard. The Fiat empire immediately decided to let Lancia contest the Safari without Fiat interfering and Mike Parkes embarked on an intensive programme of testing, mainly in East Africa, to make the Stratos a winner on the rough. The biggest problem was that which had defeated Alpine Renault on rallies like the Safari and the Bandama Rally in the past; a rear-engined car tends to suck in its own dust to the engine with dire results. The Safari turned out to be a classic and showed how well the test programme had gone, for three of these 'racing' cars were entered and three finished with Munari and Waldegaard taking second and third places overall. Waldegaard dominated a very dusty Acropolis, setting fastest time on nearly every special stage until dust seeped into the distributor through an unnoticed hole and he was out.

Above: This is how it should look. Sandro Munari and Mario Manucci not only won the first World Championship round to be held after the Stratos was homologated but also the second when they travelled to Canada and won the 1974 Rally of the Rideau Lakes

Right: Thanks to its easily removable rear bodywork, the Lancia Stratos is occasionally seen like this. On this occasion during the 1975 East African Safari, Sandro Munari and Lofty Drews had removed it on a Peugeot taxi that failed to get out of their way in a native village. Still it makes checking the oil easy

Right: Lancia's customers have not always been as fortunate as the factory with their rally cars. This example seen here making its debut on the 1975 Circuit of Ireland with Cahal Curley and Austin Frazer, was to have every kind of problem imaginable before winning its first international, the 1976 Mintex, in the hands of Andy Dawson

Lancia then had to let Fiat do a certain number of events and they did win the Portuguese Rally, making it necessary for Lancia to come back and win the San Remo with Munari to make sure that they were World Champions for the second year running.

Thus the Stratos story is a success story and shows that with the right sort of development and back-up by service crews, even such an unlikely car can go and make the running on events where the rough and tumble generally suits the saloon car. Lancia have worked hard to get private owners to run the Stratos in competition and although the efforts of Graham Warner's Chequered Flag team have been as chequered as their flag in Britain, the Lancia importers in France have run a car for Bernard Darniche in two events and won both of them. One was the Tour de France and the other the Tour de Corse, where the works cars failed to finish due to accidents.

The serious question raised by cars of this type participating in rallies is whether or not it is good for the sport. The purists tend to think that such cars are not truly road-going cars and thus should be restricted to driving on circuits—and certainly the traffic laws and regulations that are now appearing all over Europe concerning the noise and pollution produced by motor cars tends to support their views. It may not be so far in the future that it will become impossible to run a Stratos or an Alpine on the road because it does not conform to emission control regulations, or to safety standards. The opposite view to that of the purist is that the public are attracted by sporty, rorty cars and that in any case, the saloon cars are just as noisy and have engines emitting just as much pollution as their GT brothers. Certainly, modern rallying has arrived where it is today thanks to the money that has been

spent on the rallies by various promoters, whether they be companies or national tourist boards. Such benevolence cannot be expected to continue if rallying does not attract large audiences and while firms like Lancia and Alpine Renault can provide the sort of cars that the spectators like watching, rallying can expect to continue expanding.

For the private owner who has to find ways of paying for his enjoyment of rallying, the popularity of the sport makes it easier to find help, but he is often suspicious of the works teams and their highly developed cars which he cannot afford or cannot obtain. If nothing else, the increased specialization of the sort of cars that the works teams run places their performances beyond almost anything that the private owner could hope to attain. Gone are the days when a private owner became a works driver by buying a similar car to that driven by the works team and then going out and beating them on a major rally. The nearest thing which has happened in recent years was the excellent third place overall by Tony Fowkes in the 1975 RAC Rally. Most of the private owners who cannot emulate Fowkes' performance feel that an increased importance should be attached to the rallying of standard cars, Group 1 Touring cars and Group 3 GT cars, but it is difficult to see how this can be done without reverting to that old horror, the handicap or coefficient. Certainly a private owner can make a good impression by driving a Group 1 car to numerous successes but he will be unlikely to find it very competitive on the rougher events. What one can hope for is a broadening of the media coverage to give more emphasis to the standard cars without detracting from the importance of an outright win.

Rallying is a big sport and there is plenty of room for all kinds of cars and drivers.

The Evolving Sport

Rallying is a branch of motor sport that has little restriction on either its growth or breadth of appeal. Unlike hill climbing, trials or racing, it is not rigidly tied to a specific form and in consequence it encompasses such widely differing events as the East African Safari, the Tour de France, the various World Cup rallies, the Monte Carlo Rally, and the most complex navigational events that may depend on the crew finding a marshal hidden up a tree or inside a house. There is even a branch of rallying known as 'armchair rallying' where the participant does not even have to leave his own home and can compete in front of his own hearth. The most famous—or should it be infamous?—of such rallies is the St Valentine's Day Massacre which takes place every February 14th and attracts over 1400 entries from all over the World. On that day, the entrants receive an envelope through the post containing road maps of the USA and sufficient mind blowing problems of route finding to keep them busy for the next six months.

Such 'rallies' are not quite what this book was created to discuss, but their presence in the spectrum of rallying does give some idea of the appeal that the sport is capable of making to the competitive instinct in all of us. Part of the mentality of the person that dreams up such things as the Massacre belongs to the rally organizer who runs more conventional events. It must be understood that they are 'competing' as much as the men who drive in the rally cars. They are setting problems to the rally crew which may equally well be in the form

Preceding pages:
Walter Rohrl's Opel Kadett GTE in the 1975 San Remo Rally

Left: since they un-wisely closed their competitions depart-ment in 1970, British Leyland have rather been the outsiders in rallying. Brian Culcheth and Johnstone Syer have been their stal-warts, finishing second overall on the 1970 World Cup with a Triumph 2.5Pl, and then concentrating on British events with cars such as this Dolomite. At the end of 1975, BL stepped up their rally activities, announcing a programme built around a Triumph TR7

Above: Will Sparrow's Vauxhall Magnum on a typical RAC Rally sta-tely home special stage, Bramham Park, in 1975. While these stages are out of char-acter with the forest stages which are the foundation of the event, they do make it possible for large numbers of spectators to see the cars in action

of brain teasers, or a snowy road, or indeed a river swollen by rain, and it is their hope that at least some of the rally competitors may find the problem too great for them. Monsieur Garot who used to be the mastermind behind the high average speeds and the rough roads of the Liege-Sofia-Liege often said that for him the best result should be to have just a single finisher. He did get it down to seven one year but his rally was never so severe as to realise his dream. But for him and his helpers, the spirit of providing a rally which might just have that sort of result made the job of running such a large scale affair much more pleasant.

Dedication is often what is needed, for few rally organizers are profes-sionals in the sense of the rally stars that compete in them. The two top North American events—the Rally of the Rideau Lakes in Canada and

Michigan's Press-on-Regardless—were both included in the 1974 World Rally Championship and yet the men that devised them and the helpers that ran them were volunteers, giving their time and experience for no better reward than being involved in a major rally. Both are now missing from the international calendar; the Rideau Lakes from the discovery that while Canada could afford the Olym-pics it could not finance a bigger and better international car rally, and the Press-on-Regardless from the dis-covery that sometimes amateur organizers cannot understand the naked desire to win in a commercially backed factory team. World rallying is the poorer for having lost them and fortunately there are already signs that twin phoenixes may be struggling to rise from the ashes. There are plenty of signs that the traumatic coming-together of European and American

147

rally cultures has envigorated both of them and in America the special stage is here to stay. What is needed now is the commercial enterprise to handle such rallies—a lot may be learned from Europe where rally organizers compete against one another to try and produce the best rally.

Typical of these is Cesar Torres who in a very short space of time advanced the Portuguese Rally from obscurity as an event on the social calendar of the Sports Club of TAP Airways to a World Championship Rally renowned for its tough route, accurate timing and excellent paper-

If the Stratos is the beast in the Lancia stable, then this is the beauty. The Beta Coupe seen here in the hands of Simo Lampinen and Solve Andreasson during the 1974 Lombard RAC Rally. The stage is the sewage works at Esholt

outside Bradford and provides a good example of how spectators can get in on the action without getting the action in on them

work. It is men like Torres who seek to please the competitors by providing a top quality rally who have also set the pace in persuading sponsors to support their rally and thus enable them to spend money attracting the best rally cars and drivers to their events. Some rallies are international in name only with just a sprinkling of foreign drivers but others have gone to the point of virtually paying people to appear. Starting money is not quite the order of the day, however, and incentives to compete are usually made in kind. The Acropolis Rally used to offer air tickets to for-

This immaculate BMW 2002 competing on the 1000 Lakes Rally of 1974 was one of the fastest rally cars of the decade. With BMW's own sixteen valve Formula Two fuel-injected, two-litre engine, it had over 245bhp and unrivalled torque in its class. Its leading exponent was Achim Warmbold here driving with Jean Todt

They say that Alfred Hitchcock likes to appear in his own films, so perhaps you will excuse this photograph of Rauno Aaltonen and John Davenport in a works 3-litre BMW Coupe on the 1972 Olympia Rally. Sad to say this fast and beautiful piece of machinery swallowed all its water in the second half of the event and had to retire, but not before Aaltonen had relived his days at the wheel of an Austin-Healey 3000 when power was power and all that . . .

eign competitors while the Marlboro Arctic Rally paid for their hotel rooms and the Safari organizers negotiated air freight deals to get European cars out to their rally.

The effect of drawing major sponsors into rallying, once the domain of the private owner, has meant that the rallies and the rallymen themselves have had to change considerably and have become more conscious of providing a spectacle and of promoting themselves. No longer do major rallies start in the middle of the night on some deserted heath, as if they had private business with the witches in Macbeth. Perhaps the RAC Rally went a bit too far when it started in the King's Road area of London but its organizers have always shown

Les Francais ont arrivé en Amerique. The performance of the Renault 17TS in the 1974 Press-on-Regardless tended to get overlooked in the discord about the Lancias and Fiats. Jean-Luc Therier took this example to first overall

Stig Blomqvist making a splash as he takes the Saab 99EMS to a debut victory in the 1976 Boucles de Spa

Following pages: most successful Stratos in private hands has been the Chardonnet car, which contributed valuable points to Lancia's 1975 championship score. Photograph shows Bernard Darniche and Alain Mahé taking it to victory in the 1976 Lyon-Charbonnieres rally

a decent respect for publicity by starting and finishing in a civilized place at a civilized time. For the rally driver, it has meant the adoption of a style of dress which is at one and the same time practical, neat and presents the sponsor's message. The days are past when rally drivers appeared in sporting garb more appropriate to beagling or to pub-crawling. Ever since Paddy Hopkirk put a specially designed and reasonably priced rally jacket on the market back in 1965, the rally jacket industry has produced such a wide variety of styles and colours that today, each man may have his own. Underneath the rally jacket most crews wear some form of protective overalls, which are produced in a wide variety of styles and colours. In just

the same way that the rally cars are covered with slogans proclaiming brand allegiance, the drivers carry such information as their names, blood group and source of income for rallying. One of the best examples of this are the Lancia-Alitalia team whose green and white cars are matched by green and white jackets for drivers and mechanics alike, thus presenting a smart corporate image for the entire team.

The total effect of all this has been to make rallying a well presented sport and the public has responded by showing increased interest. Perhaps the most important factor in this relationship with the public has been that rallying takes motor sport to the people in a very direct manner. By virtue of using the public road, a rally may be seen by many more people than could ever be packed into a single stadium. However, such an audience is often watching the rally not by choice but by accident and it is for this reason that a lot of work is being done to make sure that it does not antagonise members of the public who may not already be fans. In most European countries, strict laws are in force regarding the noise emitted by rally cars and their comportment on the public road, thus making sure that they reserve their fireworks for the special stages where there is no other traffic. Even the previously liberal French Gendarmerie has clamped down on unnecessary speeding and in 1973 opened their campaign by insisting that the Monte Carlo Rally organizers penalise many crews caught out in traffic offences. It is for reasons like this that events in Africa and South America may well assume an even greater role in future world class rallying, but for the sponsor, the European arena is where he wants exposure for his product and it is here that the mainspring of rallying must continue.

When the public actively go to watch a rally, they can feel that they are close to the action and can even participate in it. This association is strongest when they can see the cars in service points where the drivers and mechanics work right in front of them on the side of the road. Even more intimate is the case where they may see a rally car leave the road on a special stage and they rush to push it back again! The fact that the competing cars are mainly similar cars to their own helps to reinforce this association and make them feel much more part of the sport than just passive spectators. Little distance separates the rally driver from his public and this helps to make even the superstars of the sport easily approachable for a chat or an autograph. Perhaps it is the fact that he is shut up in a car for long periods with just his co-driver to talk to that makes a rally driver keen to talk to other people. Certainly a large proportion of them are articulate and amusing to a greater audience on radio and television.

With rallying seen as an expanding sport and the upper echelons of it becoming as gilded and as expensive as Formula 1 racing, it is necessary to ask where it will find sufficient competitors to maintain it at other levels considering the mounting cost of any form of motoring. The root of the answer seems to be that it is such a diverse sport that anyone who is bitten by the bug that makes a man a rallyist can find enjoyment at a level that he can afford. Provided that the use of the public road is not denied to the ordinary motorist either by law or by economics, there will be a proportion of them that will want to go rallying. The particular mutation of the sport that may appear in the future might be unrecognizable to us today, but it will surely be a contest of crew and car against the road—with the problems of the road no doubt aided by a helpful rally organizer.

Aseptogyl dentrifice may keep your teeth clean but it does not guarantee to keep the car clean. This Group 1 Peugeot 504 has been driven across Africa to the Ivory Coast by Claudine Trautmann and Marie-Pierre Palayer to compete in the Bandama Rally and when they finished that gruelling event, why they just drove it back to France again. Tough, these French birds—and the cars stand the pace too.

One of the most tenacious Safari drivers, Joginder Singh, on his way to his second victory in the event, partnered by David Doig in 1974, in a Colt Lancer GSR which he prepared in his own Nairobi workshops. He first won the event in 1965, sharing an ex-works Volvo PV544 with his brother Jaswant Singh, and won again with Doig in 1976. His Safari record also includes second placings in 1969 (Volvo 142S) and 1970 (Datsun 1600SSS), a class win with a VW 1200 in 1960, and finishing in one of the Lincoln Mercury Comets in 1964

Index